"Father Paul Turner has given us another excellent commentary and pastoral review to the second edition of *Holy Communion and Worship of the Eucharistic Mystery outside of Mass.* Turner cites original 1972 'schemas,' *Eucharisticum Mysterium*, and other historical materials to support the theology of this edition. Turner's background as a translator for the International Commission on English in the Liturgy, gives him an advantage in translating it into everyday language, allowing people to learn the best ways to implement it for appropriate eucharistic devotions and practices."

— Very Reverend John Thomas Lane, SSS, Provincial Superior, Province of Saint Ann (USA), Congregation of the Blessed Sacrament

"The release of any new liturgical text affords a golden opportunity to provide formation and to examine pastoral practice. Father Turner offers us both in *Eucharistic Reservation.* Once again, he delivers what we have come to expect from this liturgical scholar and devoted pastor. With genuine respect for liturgical history and unbroken tradition, he explores how words and praxis have evolved over the centuries. In scholarly detail, he cross-references orations, readings, and rubrics with Scripture, other liturgical books, and Church documents. His book closely parallels the liturgical text so that all ministers may more carefully and correctly prepare the various rites."

— Rita A. Thiron, Executive Director, Federation of Diocesan Liturgical Commissions

Eucharistic Reservation

Holy Communion and Worship of the Eucharistic Mystery outside Mass

Paul Turner

LITURGICAL PRESS
Collegeville, Minnesota

litpress.org

Published by Liturgical Press, Collegeville, Minnesota. Printed in the United States of America.

Library of Congress Cataloging-in-Publication Data

Names: Turner, Paul, 1953– author.
Title: Eucharistic reservation : Holy communion and worship of the eucharistic mystery outside mass / Paul Turner.
Description: Collegeville, Minnesota : Liturgical Press, [2024] | Summary: "In Eucharistic Reservation, Paul Turner explains the new translation of Holy Communion and Worship of the Eucharistic Mystery outside Mass, a text that provides guidelines for eucharistic adoration and communion services for those unable to participate in the sacrifice of the Mass"—Provided by publisher.
Identifiers: LCCN 2023043813 (print) | LCCN 2023043814 (ebook) | ISBN 9798400800894 (trade paperback) | ISBN 9798400800900 (epub) | ISBN 9798400801327 (pdf)
Subjects: LCSH: Catholic Church. Holy Communion and worship of the Eucharist outside Mass. | Lord's Supper—Reservation—Catholic Church. | BISAC: RELIGION / Christian Rituals & Practice / Worship & Liturgy | RELIGION / Christianity / Catholic
Classification: LCC BX2045.H553 T87 2024 (print) | LCC BX2045.H553 (ebook) | DDC 264/.36—dc23/eng/20231122
LC record available at https://lccn.loc.gov/2023043813
LC ebook record available at https://lccn.loc.gov/2023043814

QVATTVOR DECENNORIVM SERVITII SEDVLI
PRO POPVLO PLVS FIDEI EVCHARISTICÆ
QVAM SACERDOTVM EVCHARISTIÆ GRATIA
DEDICAT AVCTOR HOC VOLVMEN SOBRINÆ SVÆ
MARIÆ BERTRANDI

Contents

Acknowledgments ix

Abbreviations xi

Revival 1

General Introduction 28

Holy Communion outside Mass 33

Administration of Communion and Viaticum to the Sick by an Extraordinary Minister 75

Various Forms of Worship of the Most Holy Eucharist 94

Eucharistic Reservations 154

Summary 177

Acknowledgments

I wish to thank

The Benedictines who celebrate and worship the Eucharist,

The missionaries who give their body and blood,

The International Commission on English in the Liturgy, which archives,

Members of the Body of Christ who spend one hour with the Lord,

God, who reveals the eucharistic mystery.

P.T.

Abbreviations

CB	*Ceremonial of Bishops* (Collegeville, MN: Liturgical Press, 1989)
CCC	*Catechism of the Catholic Church*, Second Edition (Vatican City: Libreria Editrice Vaticana, 1997)
EM	Sacred Congregation of Rites, *Eucharisticum Mysterium*, 1967
GIRM	The General Instruction of the Roman Missal, Revised Edition (Washington, DC: United States Conference of Catholic Bishops, 2011)
HC	*Holy Communion and Worship of the Eucharistic Mystery outside Mass* (Collegeville, MN: Liturgical Press, 2024)
ICEL	The International Commission on English in the Liturgy
OM	The Order of Mass in the Roman Missal
PCS	Pastoral Care of the Sick: Rites of Anointing and Viaticum, *The Rites*, Volume I (Collegeville, MN: Liturgical Press, 1990).
SC	The Second Vatican Council, *Sacrosanctum Concilium* (Constitution on the Sacred Liturgy), 1963
USCCB	The United States Conference of Catholic Bishops

Revival

A Moment in History

Interest in eucharistic reservation increased among Catholics in the early twenty-first century for two reasons: the shortage of priests to celebrate Mass and the plenitude of devotion to the enduring sacramental presence of Christ. The *Catechism of the Catholic Church* notes the uniqueness of the real presence of Christ under the forms of bread and wine in the eucharistic species of his Body and Blood (CCC 1374) and that this presence endures from the moment of consecration as long as the two species subsist (1377). This belief explains the historic devotion to the part of the Mass when the consecration occurs, as well as various practices pertaining to reserving consecrated hosts after Mass in tabernacles.

Even as this resurgent devotion led to a greater demand for eucharistic adoration, a survey of Catholic belief turned the heads of complacent leaders.[1] With headlines claiming that only a third of Catholics believe in the real presence of Christ in the Eucharist, Pew Research Center appraised belief with an irresponsible question: "Which is the Catholic teaching about bread and wine in Communion? They become [the] actual body and blood of Christ, they are symbols of the body and blood of Christ."[2]

[1] Gregory A. Smith, "Just One-Third of U.S. Catholics Agree with Their Church That the Eucharist Is Body, Blood of Christ," Pew Research Center, August 5, 2019, https://www.pewresearch.org/fact-tank/2019/08/05/transubstantiation-eucharist-u-s-catholics/.

[2] Pew Research Center, "What Americans Know About Religion," July 23, 2019, https://www.pewresearch.org/religion/2019/07/23/what-americans-know-about-religion/.

Neither of these options faithfully represents the belief of Catholics, making it impossible for even the most devout believer to answer accurately. The catechism does not speak of the "actual body and blood of Christ." It speaks of the real presence of Christ. If "actual" means the diagnostically physical flesh and blood of Jesus of Nazareth, then Catholics do not believe in that kind of presence. They believe in the presence of the risen Christ. The catechism reassures believers that "the breaking of bread does not divide Christ" (CCC 1377), something that one might fear if communion were the "actual" body of Christ.

Furthermore, many interpreted the second option as belief that the bread and wine are "just symbols," even though the word "just" does not appear in the question. The General Instruction of the Roman Missal calls the Eucharist "a symbol of that one body of which [Christ] is the head" (GIRM 5). It is not "just a symbol," but a very meaningful symbol that expresses authentic Catholic belief.

In spite of its flaws, the survey alarmed many Church leaders who read the headlines, not the question. In 2022 the United States Conference of Catholic Bishops launched a three-year National Eucharistic Revival "to restore understanding and devotion to this great mystery here in the United States by helping us renew our worship of Jesus Christ in the Eucharist."[3] In support of this focus, the revival has fostered graphics pertaining to moments such as the consecration during the eucharistic prayer, eucharistic reservation in tabernacles, and the adoration of a consecrated host set within a monstrance. By contrast, the eucharistic revival that the Second Vatican Council promoted in its Constitution on the Sacred Liturgy pertained not to "understanding and devotion," but more to

[3] US Conference of Catholic Bishops, National Eucharistic Revival, https://www.eucharisticrevival.org/.

the "full and active participation by all the people" in the Mass, which it called the "paramount concern" (SC 14).[4]

Into this moment of history comes a revised English translation of the Vatican's 1973 compilation of rites pertaining to the reservation of the Eucharist, *Holy Communion and Worship of the Eucharistic Mystery outside Mass* (HC).[5] Published in 2024, it replaces the first translation from 1976. Part of the long process of updating the vernacular translations of the original Latin orders of service in order to adhere to new rules, this project came into the ambit of the International Commission on English in the Liturgy.[6]

Early History

Eucharistic reservation has been practiced since the early days of the Church, at first in order to supply communion to the faithful outside Mass. In the mid-second century, Justin the Martyr reported that deacons in Rome brought communion to the faithful who were absent from the Eucharist. The practice demonstrated belief in the enduring presence of Christ in eucharistic species and the organic link between communion and the community's celebration of the Eucharist.[7] At the turn of the third century, Tertullian of Carthage reported that Christians took home some of the bread consecrated on Sunday and

[4] Austin Flannery, ed., *Vatican Council II: Constitutions, Decrees, Declarations; The Basic Sixteen Documents* (Collegeville, MN: Liturgical Press, 2014), p. 124.

[5] *Holy Communion and Worship of the Eucharistic Mystery outside Mass* (Collegeville, MN: Liturgical Press, 2024).

[6] The author serves as a facilitator for this organization's meetings, taking notes, writing reports, and recalling past discussions so that the bishops may concentrate more fully on the work at hand.

[7] Robert Cabié, *The Church at Prayer: An Introduction to the Liturgy*, ed. Aimé Georges Martimort, vol. 2, *The Eucharist*, trans. Matthew J. O'Connell (Collegeville, MN: Liturgical Press, 1986), p. 235, citing the *First Apology*, chap. 67.

gave themselves communion during the week.[8] St. Basil the Great (†379) permitted desert ascetics to retain the Eucharist in order to give themselves communion.[9] By the fourth or fifth century, the *Apostolic Tradition* further encouraged the faithful to store carefully the communion bread that they had brought home and to eat it prior to their meals.[10] This aimed to protect the consecrated bread from spoiling and to arrange its consumption apart from ordinary food.

Encouragement to adore the sacrament while receiving communion began by the fourth century. Cyril of Jerusalem (†386), in a passage showing the antiquity of receiving communion in the hand, encouraged those approaching the minister holding the Body of Christ to present their hands one on top of the other to make a throne, and to bow before the chalice of the Blood of Christ in the manner of one who worships.[11] Augustine (†430), bishop of Hippo in North Africa, commenting on Psalm 99, declared that no one eats the Body of Christ without first worshiping it,[12] though this may refer more to an attitude of faith than any ritual act. By 700, at the end of the eucharistic prayer at a papal Mass, the archdeacon lifted the chalice toward the pope, who touched it with the vessel holding the other offerings.[13] Thus, ceremonial elements were entering the celebration of the Eucharist to show the honor due to the consecrated Body and Blood of Christ.

[8] Philippe Rouillard, "The Viaticum," in *Handbook for Liturgical Studies, Volume III: The Eucharist*, ed. Anscar J. Chupungco (Collegeville, MN: Liturgical Press, 1999), p. 288, citing *On Prayer*, chap. 19.

[9] Edward Foley, *Eucharistic Adoration after Vatican II* (Collegeville, MN: Liturgical Press, 2022), p. 4.

[10] Nathan D. Mitchell, "Worship of the Eucharist Outside Mass," in *Handbook for Liturgical Studies*, p. 267, citing *Apostolic Tradition*, chaps. 36–37.

[11] Rouillard, p. 268, citing *Catecheses* V. 21–22.

[12] Rouillard, p. 268, citing *Enarrationes in Psalmos* 99:9, though 99:8 in some translations.

[13] Rouillard, p. 269, citing *Ordo Romanus I*: 74–108, found in 89–90.

Adoring the reserved sacrament outside the liturgy developed only later. By the twelfth century, for example, a rule of life for women living near a church urged them to make gestures and offer words of adoration. From their cells they were to turn their thoughts toward the Body and Blood of Christ on the altar of the church, fall on their knees in that direction, and greet the One who provides food for the journey of life.[14]

Eucharistic processions multiplied after the establishment of the feast of Corpus Christi in 1264, a universal celebration of belief in the real and enduring presence of Christ in the eucharistic species. These provided points of gathering for people living in towns, stirred their devotion, and challenged dissidents.[15] They also afforded the pleasures of spectacle and festivity.

The practice of eucharistic exposition and Benediction emerged shortly later. Since the twelfth century, the priest at Mass was elevating the host at the consecration for the adoration of the people. A few centuries later he lifted the chalice for the same purpose. As church authorities were not offering the people communion from the chalice out of fears of spilling the Precious Blood, the faithful focused their attention on the consecrated host. Some parishes featured a dark cloth draped behind the altar to improve visibility, a candle lifted by a server for illumination, or the ringing of a bell as an aural cue.[16]

For those who felt unworthy of the sacrament, viewing the host substituted for receiving communion. This "ocular communion" spread to the point where some of the faithful erroneously believed that seeing the host was tantamount to consuming it. Some reportedly did not stay for the end of the

[14] Rouillard, p. 272, citing M. B. Salu, ed., *The Ancrene Riwle* (London: 1955), 7.

[15] Rouillard, p. 273.

[16] Rouillard, pp. 273–74. Ed Foley, *From Age to Age: How Christians Have Celebrated the Eucharist* (Collegeville, MN: Liturgical Press, 2008), pp. 198 and 225.

celebration because they had achieved the goal of their devotion.[17] (The same phenomenon occurred during and after the worst of the COVID-19 pandemic, when the faithful watched Mass and exposition of the Blessed Sacrament from screens at home. Even when civil law permitted a return to public places, some Catholics kept substituting participation at Mass with its contemporary ocular equivalent, even defending its spiritual benefits.[18])

These practices led to exposing the Blessed Sacrament outside Mass. Some evening devotions in fourteenth-century Italy took place in the presence of the exposed Sacrament, and the priest sometimes concluded the liturgy by blessing the people with the vessel containing the consecrated host. This practice also developed at stations in eucharistic processions. Eventually the celebration of Benediction with the Blessed Sacrament took on such splendor that it exceeded the attention given a Low Mass that featured less sumptuous vestments, no singing or preaching, and few communicants.[19]

The Roman Ritual of 1614 provided a service for administering Holy Communion outside Mass.[20] The priest processed toward the altar, opened the tabernacle situated there, removed the vessel with hosts, and set it on a corporal atop the altar. He addressed the people from the side of the altar so he would never turn his back on the Sacrament. He led them in a brief general confession. He raised one host over the ciborium and declared in Latin, "Behold, the Lamb of God, behold him who

[17] Rouillard, pp. 273–74. John Thomas Lane, *Guide for Celebrating: Worship of the Eucharist Outside Mass* (Chicago: Liturgy Training Publications, 2015), p. 7.

[18] Betty Anne Asaro, "The Powerful, Prayerful Experience of Being a Remote Parishioner," *America*, December 9, 2022, https://www.americamagazine.org/faith/2022/12/09/virtual-mass-prayer-people-god-244158.

[19] Rouillard, pp. 274–75.

[20] Anthony Ward and Cuthbert Johnson, eds., *Rituale Romanum*, Editio prima post typicam anno 1953 promulgata, Titulus V, Caput II (Rome: CLV Edizioni Liturgiche, 2001), pp. 154–58.

takes away the sins of the world." He continued in Latin, saying three times the formula later assigned to the people, "Lord, I am not worthy that you should enter under my roof, but only say the word and my soul shall be healed." (Many Catholics did not know enough Latin to say the words.) He distributed communion using the Latin formula then in force: "May the Body of our Lord Jesus Christ protect your soul for eternal life. Amen." Returning the vessel to the altar, he recited the words of the Corpus Christi antiphon *O sacrum convivium* (now HC 200). He led the verse *Panem de cælo*, and a server offered the response; both parts concerning the gift of bread from heaven came from the concluding rites of the eucharistic procession for Corpus Christi in the *Liber Usualis*, where they also reappeared before the final prayer at Lauds and second Vespers for the same day. The priest recited a prayer, purified his fingers, and blessed the people. A deacon could conduct the same ceremony outside Mass.

A priest conducted the same ritual *during* Mass to offer communion to the people.[21] The preconciliar missal's Order of Mass included only the communion of the priest. If people were also to receive, after the priest received communion, he interrupted the Order of Mass and conducted the above ceremony, withdrawing hosts from the tabernacle and beginning with the general confession. In 1947, Pope Pius XII encouraged people to receive communion after the priest, preferably from hosts consecrated at the same Mass, rather than from the tabernacle,[22] an important change that never fully took root in Catholic parochial practice. (Even today, many parishes retain the habits of the past: The priest consecrates a host for himself and perhaps a portion of the people. The rest receive communion from previously consecrated hosts in the tabernacle, as if participating in a communion service outside Mass.)

[21] *Rituale Romanum*, Titulus V, Caput II:11, p. 158.

[22] Pope Pius XII, *Mediator Dei: On the Sacred Liturgy*, pars. 121–22, https://www.papalencyclicals.net/pius12/p12media.htm.

In spite of the grassroots popularity of exposition of the Blessed Sacrament and Benediction, the Roman Ritual of 1614 contained no order of service for it. Only in 1927 did a ceremony based on the eighteenth-century instructions of Popes Clement VII and VIII appear in a supplement of the Ritual, offering litanies and prayers for exposition and reposition of the Most Blessed Sacrament for the devotion called "Forty Hours."[23] The practice originated in the late medieval period on Holy Thursday, when the faithful gathered at the conclusion of the Mass to keep vigil before the Blessed Sacrament for the forty hours that elapsed from the close of the service to the celebration of Easter.[24] Augustine had noted that Jesus rose on Sunday forty hours after his death on Friday, anticipating the forty days he remained on the earth between his resurrection and ascension.[25]

The Roman Ritual gave instructions for a eucharistic procession on the feast of Corpus Christi, the Body of Christ.[26] It called for proper decoration of the church and of the public streets. The priest consecrated two hosts at Mass, consuming one and placing the other in a monstrance. He wore a white cope to kneel and incense the sacrament. He took the monstrance in hand, turned toward the people, and processed with various ministers holding an umbrella and thuribles. A cleric or the priest intoned the hymn *Pange lingua,* followed by *Tantum ergo, Sacris solemniis, Verbum supernum, Salutis humanæ, Æterne Rex,* and the *Te Deum,* the *Benedictus,* and the *Magnificat.* Upon arrival at the church, the monstrance was set upon the altar, all knelt in adoration, the priest incensed the sacrament, and the *Tantum ergo* was sung again. The clerics sang the verse

[23] *Rituale Romanum,* Titulus V, Caput VII, Litaniæ, Preces et Orationes quæ dicuntur in Expositione et Repositione SS.mi Sacramenti pro Oratione XL Horarum, pp. 166–79.

[24] Lane, p. 6.

[25] Augustine, *On the Trinity,* book 4, chap. 6, n. 10, cited by Lane, p. 6.

[26] *Rituale Romanum,* Titulus X, Caput V, De Processione in Festo SS.mi Corporis Christi, pp. 803–12.

and response *Panem de cælo*, and the priest offered several prayers. Genuflecting, he took the monstrance in hand and blessed the people with the sign of the cross, saying nothing. Finally, he reposed the Blessed Sacrament.

The rituals pertaining to eucharistic reservation appeared in three disparate parts of the Roman Ritual, reflecting the historical evolution of these practices: distributing communion outside Mass, Forty Hours Devotion, and eucharistic processions. As the liturgical renewal of the twentieth century took shape, the interrelation of these rituals became more evident because they pertained to the purposes of eucharistic reservation—the distribution of Holy Communion and worship of the Blessed Sacrament. Another feature uniting them was their distinction from the celebration of the Mass. In the past, pastoral practices obscured this unity by distributing all the faithful's Holy Communion from the tabernacle during Mass and developing ritual actions pertaining to eucharistic worship during Mass. In the reforms, the Church reframed its thinking about the Eucharist, which had a profound effect on other aspects of the liturgy. Many Catholics think that the liturgical renewal accomplished two goals: Mass in the vernacular and the priest facing the people. However, the revised liturgy accomplished something more: a refinement of the doctrine of the Eucharist and its implications for the celebration of the Mass and the derivative practices of eucharistic reservation.

Eucharisticum Mysterium

The Second Vatican Council's Constitution on the Sacred Liturgy, *Sacrosanctum Concilium*, elaborated a theology of the Mass in 1963. Jesus Christ instituted the sacrifice of his Body and Blood and entrusted the memorial of his death and resurrection to the Church (SC 47). The faithful are to take part in the action, fully conscious, with devotion and collaboration (48). Notably, echoing the admonition of Pope Pius XII, "The more perfect form of participation in the Mass whereby the faithful, after the priest's communion, receive the Lord's body from the same sacrifice, is warmly commended" (55).[27] Receiving communion from the bread and wine consecrated at the altar during Mass is more perfect than receiving communion from the tabernacle. By stating the central purpose of the altar of sacrifice, the council clarified the derivative purpose of the tabernacle.

The Sacred Congregation of Rites issued the instruction *Eucharisticum Mysterium* (EM) in 1967, part of a series of documents to aid the implementation of the liturgical reforms. Even before the 1969 revised Order of Mass with its missal and lectionary, the congregation sought to clarify and purify the preservation of eucharistic devotion in its relationship to the Mass.

The instruction opens with a declaration: "The eucharistic mystery is truly the center of the liturgy and indeed of the whole Christian life" (EM 1).[28] Its introduction summarizes important doctrinal themes:

- In the Mass, the faithful, the Body of Christ, participate in the sacrifice of Christ and its memorial while sharing in the sacred banquet of his Body and Blood.
- The Mass is both sacrifice and sacred meal.
- The Mass is both the action of Christ and of the Church.
- No Mass is a private act, but a celebration of the Church in its orders and ministries in which all have an active part.
- The Mass is the origin and purpose of worship of the Eucharist outside Mass.
- Christ is to be adored in the reserved sacrament.

[27] *Vatican Council II*, pp. 136–37.

[28] Sacred Congregation of Rites, *Eucharisticum Mysterium* (On Worship of the Eucharist), Instruction, May 25, 1967, in *The Liturgy Documents*, vol. 3, *Foundational Documents on the Origins and Implementation of* Sacrosanctum Concilium (Chicago: Liturgy Training Publications, 2013), p. 381.

- Both the Mass and worship of the reserved sacrament together extend the grace of the sacrifice (EM 3).

After this introduction, the first part details general principles for catechesis on the eucharistic mystery:

- The eucharistic mystery is the center of the whole life of the Church (EM 6).
- The eucharistic mystery is the center of the local Church (EM 7).
- The memorial of the Lord brings about the unity of all who believe in him and inspires the faithful to pray for the unity of all Christians (EM 8).
- Christ is present in the assembly of the faithful, in his word, in the priest, and above all in the eucharistic elements (EM 9).
- The Liturgy of the Word and the Liturgy of the Eucharist constitute a single act of worship (EM 10).
- All the faithful belong to the royal priesthood that requires their active participation (EM 11).
- Active participation means giving thanks to God and receiving communion through inner affections and outward rites (EM 12).
- The faithful strive to live their whole lives joyfully in the strength of the heavenly food they receive (EM 13).
- Children are to receive religious instruction on the Mass (EM 14).
- The starting points for catechesis are the liturgical year and the rites and prayers of the Mass (EM 15).

The second part treats the celebration of the Mass. It opens with general norms: the unity that the participation of the people acquires (EM 16), the avoidance of two simultaneous celebrations in the same church that may distract the people (17), a sense of both local and universal Church (18), the welcoming of visitors who may need help with the regional vernacular (19), the care required for celebrating Mass with a sense of the sacred (20), proper communication of the eucharistic prayer (21), the avoidance of disturbing the faithful in attendance when Mass is broadcast (22), the avoidance of distraction by photographers (23), and the careful arrangement of churches, their furnishings and vestments (24).

This second part continues with specific concerns for Sundays and weekdays. The Eucharist is most expressive when celebrated on the day that Jesus rose from the dead (EM 25), and when the bishop in his cathedral or the pastor in his parish presides over a celebration with music for the assembly (26). Masses for particular groups within parishes are best arranged on weekdays or as part of parish celebrations on Sundays and holy days (27). Sunday and holy day Masses may be anticipated the previous evening at a time determined by the ordinary (28). The faithful are encouraged to participate in Mass on weekdays, especially during Lent and Advent (29). Gatherings for spiritual congresses or retreats fittingly make the celebration of the Eucharist their high point (30).

This same second part of EM addresses the communion of the faithful. The faithful participate more fully in the Mass when they receive communion at the prescribed time, immediately after the priest receives, and from hosts consecrated at the same Mass (EM 31). As the sign of Holy Communion is more complete when one receives it under both kinds, the circumstances permitting sharing the chalice with the faithful have increased (32). The faithful are to receive communion during Mass, but they may receive communion outside Mass when necessary, even in the afternoon, which had formerly been restricted (33). The conference of bishops establishes the posture for receiving communion, either kneeling as a sign of adoration or standing and performing an additional sign of reverence (34). Although the Eucharist frees one from daily faults, those aware of mortal sin are to make a sacramental confession prior to receiving communion (35). The faithful beginning a new state or way of apostolic service fittingly take part in a Mass and receive communion (36). Priests are to exhort the people to frequent or daily reception of communion (37). To prolong the benefits of the sacrament in one's daily life, the faithful are encouraged to remain in church for some time of prayer after receiving communion (38). The faithful in danger of death are required to receive communion as Viaticum while they are in full possession of their faculties (39). Communion may be brought to those unable to come to church, such as the sick and elderly (40). Those unable to consume bread may receive communion under the form of wine with permission of the bishop (41).

The second part of EM concludes with a section on the celebration of the Eucharist in the life of the priest. When the bishop presides, the Mass manifests the unity and order of the Church (EM 42). Priests are to fulfill the office proper to them by celebrating or concelebrating Mass, rather than by receiving communion as the laity do (43). The priest is urged to celebrate Mass daily, even when the faithful cannot attend (44). Priests are to preside according to the norm of law and not make changes by a presumed private authority (45). Priests are to ensure the participation of the faithful, choosing the forms of celebration that suit them best (46). Concelebration expresses the unity of the sacrifice and of the priesthood (47). If a large host is baked for concelebration, its form is to be worthy of the eucharistic mystery (48).

The third major part of EM concerns worship of the Eucharist as an enduring sacrament. This part especially laid the foundation for the liturgical book *Holy Communion and Worship of the Eucharistic Mystery outside Mass* (HC). The first section presents reasons for reserving the sacrament outside Mass. The primary purpose of eucharistic reservation is to provide Viaticum to the dying, and secondarily for communion outside

Mass and adoration of Jesus Christ (EM 49). Those adoring the sacrament are to remember that the presence of Christ derives from the sacrifice that has both sacramental and spiritual communion as its purpose (50). Those responsible for places where the sacrament is reserved are to keep them open at convenient hours for the faithful to go and pray (51).

The second section of the third part addresses the place for eucharistic adoration, and it shows some of the early conflicting opinions over the relationship between the tabernacle and the celebration of the Mass. Each church should have one secure tabernacle for eucharistic reservation (EM 52). A separate chapel is recommended to facilitate the private prayer of the people, so as not to distract from celebrations at the main altar (53). Citing 1964 legislation, the tabernacle is to be placed on the main altar or another worthy altar, even where Mass is celebrated facing the people (54). However, due to the various modes of Christ's presence, it is more in keeping with the Mass that the reserved sacrament not be kept in a tabernacle on the altar where Mass is celebrated because Christ becomes present as a result of the consecration (55). The construction of new churches (56) is to comply with numbers 52 and 54, and the remodeling of existing churches is to observe number 24. To alert the faithful to the presence of the Blessed Sacrament, a veil or some other object identifies the tabernacle, and a lamp burns continuously as a sign of honor (57).

The third section briefly addresses approved eucharistic devotions. These are encouraged in accord with the council's concern about the relationship between the liturgy and nonliturgical sacred services that harmonize with the seasons, derive from the liturgy, and lead people toward them because the Mass surpasses any devotion (EM 58). Among these, the fourth section notes, are eucharistic processions. Carrying the Blessed Sacrament through the streets as advised by the local ordinary, especially on the feast of Corpus Christi, the faithful bear witness to their devotion (59).

The fifth section concerns exposition of the Blessed Sacrament, which draws the faithful to an awareness of the sublime presence of Christ. Still, it must carefully correlate with the Mass because Christ instituted the Eucharist to feed, heal, and comfort (EM 60). In a change to prevailing tradition, Mass was not to be celebrated in the presence of the exposed Sacrament for reasons suggested in number 55, and because Mass is the higher way of inner communion toward which exposition leads (61). Exposition may be on the altar or a throne, and the faithful spend time before the sacrament with private prayer, hearing Scripture and a homily or reflection, in song and silence, concluding with Benediction and a hymn such as *Tantum ergo* or a vernacular hymn approved by the conference of bishops (62). Churches with the reserved sacrament may arrange an annual time of extended exposition (63). Where the faithful come in large numbers, the local ordinary may order prolonged exposition and prayer (64). If necessary, prolonged exposition may be interrupted, the priest replacing the Sacrament in the tabernacle at fixed times up to twice a day (65). Short expositions should still allow time for readings from Scripture, hymns, prayers, and silence, and may never take place solely to give Benediction after Mass (66).

The third section concludes with a note about eucharistic congresses. Such gatherings help the faithful understand the eucharistic mystery through private prayers, devotions, and solemn processions, but their culmination is the celebration of the Mass (EM 67).

In 1967, even before releasing a revised Order of Mass, the Vatican articulated principles of eucharistic theology, the importance of the Mass, and the relative places of communion outside Mass and worship of the Blessed Sacrament. These principles set the groundwork for HC, the liturgical book that governs the practice of Catholic eucharistic devotion apart from, but derived from and leading back toward, the Mass.

Administering Communion outside Mass

The Vatican privately distributed its first draft of a revised rite for administering communion outside Mass in 1969.[29] The apostolic delegate to the United States, Archbishop Luigi Raimondi, sent a letter to the president of the National Conference of Catholic Bishops (NCCB), Cardinal John Dearden, providing the Latin original of the revised 1969 instruction *Fidei Custos,* which authorized the establishment of lay ministers of Holy Communion. Presumably, similar delegates sent similar letters to other conferences of bishops.

This "Instruction concerning Extraordinary Ministers for Administering Holy Eucharistic Communion" included two attachments approved by the Vatican's Consilium for Implementing the Constitution on the Sacred Liturgy, both in Latin: "The Rite for Deputing a Minister Who Is Able to Distribute Holy Communion by an Apostolic Indult" and "The Rite of Administering Holy Communion by a Minister Having the Faculty from an Indult of the Apostolic See." The first is the earliest draft of the ritual, with alternatives for celebrating within and outside Mass. The version that later came into force can be found in chapter 63 of the *Book of Blessings*.[30]

The second attachment shows the foundation for what ultimately appeared in *Holy Communion and Worship of the Eucharistic Mystery outside Mass*. This entire unpublished ritual from 1969 fills only two pages:

> The Rite of Administering Holy Communion by a Minister Having the Faculty by Indult[31] of the Apostolic See

[29] In its archives, ICEL has an unpublished copy of this draft along with a cover letter from the National Council of Catholic Bishops' assistant general secretary Father Edwin Neill to Father Frederick McManus, a founding member of ICEL.

[30] *Book of Blessings* (Collegeville, MN: Liturgical Press, 1989).

[31] The indult must be requested according to the norm of the instruction *Fidei Custos* by the Sacred Congregation of Sacraments, or by the Sacred Congregation for the Evangelization of the Nations "for the sake of those subject to its authority."

I. Introduction

1. On the altar at least two candles should be lighted. The corporal should be placed on the mensa; near the tabernacle, though, should be placed a small container with water and a purificator for purifying fingers after the distribution of communion.

2. The minister who is to distribute Holy Communion washes his (her) hands and wears the appropriate vesture for this sacred mystery.

II. The Longer Rite

3. Before Holy Communion may be distributed, especially on Sundays and holydays of obligation, a sacred celebration of the Word of God takes place,[32] in almost the same structure laid down in the Liturgy of the Word at Mass: From the Mass of the day are read the epistle and the gospel, the chants, especially those from the psalms, before and between the readings.[33]

   The one who presides may read *a homily provided by the bishop or by a pastor*. Then the universal prayer or prayer of the faithful takes place.

   After the universal prayer, all recite the Lord's Prayer, and the *Confiteor*, (omitting the words "to you, Father" and "you, Father,") or the act of contrition that is used in individual regions.

   Then the minister says, "Behold the Lamb of God, behold him who takes away the sins of the world," and all immediately add, "Lord, I am not worthy that you should enter under my roof, but only say the word and my soul shall be healed."

   The minister, before distributing Holy Communion to others, may consume it himself (herself), saying

[32] Constitution on the Sacred Liturgy, article 35, 4, A. A. S. 56, 1964, p. 109. Instruction *Inter Œcumenici*, nn. 37–39; A. A. S. 56, 1964; pp. 884–85.

[33] Instruction *Inter Œcumenici*, n. 37; A. A. S. 56, 1964; pp. 884–85.

quietly, "May the Body of Christ keep me safe for eternal life. Amen."

Then he (she) distributes Holy Communion to others, saying to each, "The Body of Christ," to which they respond, "Amen."

The rite concludes with some sacred song or another prayer in thanksgiving.

III. The Brief Rite

4. Before Holy Communion may be distributed, in place of a celebration of the Word of God, there may be read, when circumstances suggest, John 6:55-57, or another short reading from sacred Scripture.

   Then the Lord's Prayer should be recited, and the other parts indicated above (n. 3) take place.

5. However, if circumstances require it, the rite may take its start directly from the Lord's Prayer. The rest should take place as indicated above (n. 3).

Although this 1969 draft was never published, other aids were. For example, a collection of provisional texts obtained from the Congregation for Divine Worship appeared in 1971. This sixteen-page booklet included rites for communion to the sick, commissioning an extraordinary minister, designating a minister of communion on a particular occasion, the administration of communion by a special minister, and texts for use outside Mass. The pamphlet credits ICEL's provisional translation from the Rites for the Sick. These bear similarities to rituals appearing later in other books, but they were all provisional—and available—at the time.[34]

[34] *The Distribution of Communion to the Sick, Rite for Commissioning an Extraordinary Minister of Holy Communion, Rite for the Designation of a Minister of Holy Communion on a Particular Occasion, Rite for Administration of Communion by a Special Minister, and Texts for the Rite Outside Mass: Rites Prepared by the Congregation for Divine Worship, Provisional Texts* (Hales Corners, WI: Priests of the Sacred Heart, 1971).

Drafts of the Revised Rite

Raimondi's letter was dated May 19, 1969, shortly after Pope Paul VI had created the Sacred Congregation for Divine Worship, folding the Consilium into it. Whereas the Consilium had been implementing the Constitution on the Sacred Liturgy, most of its work had been completed by this time, so its absorption into a new congregation simplified the procedures for continuing the liturgical renewal. Most of its work on HC was carried out over a few months in 1972.

A subcommittee accepted the charge to revise the parts of the Roman Ritual dealing with the Most Blessed Sacrament of the Eucharist and with processions. Chaired by Virgilio Noè, the undersecretary of the congregation, the group's other members were Vincenzo Raffa, Charles Michel-Jean, S.S.S., L. Vassalli, Ignazio Calabuig, and Gottardo Pasqualetti.[35] A handwritten note on one of the schemata lists Pierre Jounel as another member.[36]

According to the complete listing of hundreds of schemata for the revised liturgy, this group produced six, yet only three remain in archives. The first of the six, number 400, which is missing from archives, appears in the list with the assuredly erroneous date of January 1978. The last two, numbers 418 and 424, dated February 21 and July 19 in 1973, are also missing. However, the three that remain provide helpful information about the development of this liturgical book: schema 401 (January 25, 1972), schema 403 (February 11, 1972),[37] and schema 405 (April 20, 1972).[38]

[35] Annibale Bugnini, *The Reform of the Liturgy 1948–1975*, trans. Matthew J. O'Connell (Collegeville, MN: Liturgical Press, 1990), p. 661.

[36] Sacra Congregatio pro Cultu Divino, schema 401, "De Sacramentali Communione et De Eucharistico Cultu Extra Missam," p. 1.

[37] Sacra Congregatio pro Cultu Divino, schema 403, "De SS.ma Eucharistia, seu de sacra Communione et de cultu mysteri eucharistici extra Missam."

[38] Sacra Congregatio pro Cultu Divino, schema 405, "De SS.ma Eucharistia, seu de sacra Communione et de cultu mysteri eucharistici extra Missam."

The first of these opens with this note:

> The study group that was established to research and propose a document on Communion Outside Mass and Eucharistic Worship Toward the Enduring Sacrament has met twice so far, namely 26–29 November 1971 and 13–15 January 1972.
>
> The fruit of the work of the members of the group is contained in the present document, still imperfect, and as is obvious, needing improvements on many points.
>
> Two matters must be especially addressed:
>
> 1. *Certain doctrinal points* have been attached to the work of the consultors, which as has been unanimously admitted, are necessary in such a document. Comments on these are greatly desired at this stage of the work.
> 2. The section that is strictly normative, whether *rubrical* or ceremonial, is found here only in part. This still must be devised in a comprehensive and particular way. This will take place in the second stage of the work.[39]

After a brief introduction, the schema considers four topics: the aforementioned principles, communion outside Mass, the purpose and rite of adoration before the venerable sacrament, and eucharistic reservation.

The section on communion outside Mass subdivides under the following headings: the minister of communion outside Mass; the circumstances for communion, namely the place, time, and method of carrying the Eucharist; things required for administering communion; and fragments. It then treated matters about the person receiving communion, the eucharistic fast, and the rite to be used in the administration of communion in both a fuller and brief form, as well as its inclusion within the Liturgy of the Hours. The section concludes with notes on the communion of the sick.

[39] Schema 401, p. 1.

The third section, concerning adoration, opens with certain doctrinal points. It then presents the rite of adoration: the rite of exposition with its purpose and liturgical requirements; the rite of adoration; and the rite of Benediction with its meaning, minister and rubrics. This section also explores extraordinary forms of eucharistic worship: the feast of the Body and Blood of Christ, eucharistic processions, and eucharistic congresses. (In the nineteenth century, a feast of the Most Precious Blood of Christ had been added to the calendar to complement the traditional observance of Corpus Christi, which focused on the Body of Christ. The revised calendar expanded the title of the traditional day to embody both concepts: the solemnity of the Most Holy Body and Blood of Christ. This draft of HC reflects the new title. Although many people still refer to the day as Corpus Christi, the full title better expresses the mystery being celebrated.)

The final section of schema 401 concerns eucharistic reservation. It treats the place of reservation and the secure keeping of the species, eucharistic vessels, the tabernacle, the location of the tabernacle, and a sign of the eucharistic presence, such as a lamp.

This schema sowed seeds that helped formulate the final document; however, the group almost immediately rejected its structure. Annibale Bugnini explained that the doctrinal work it contained would have required a lengthy and complex duty. Rather than compose a new treatment, the group decided to synthesize documents that had already been published. The members entrusted this work to Carlo Braga, C.M.[40] He apparently finished his work in less than three weeks.

Schema 403 presents a revised outline that shows more clearly the marks of the final product. The cover letter explains that the document did not wish to be a new tract or instruction. It relied instead on the documents of the Second Vatican Council, Paul VI's encyclical letter *Mysterium Fidei*, and the congregation's instruction *Eucharisticum Mysterium*, as well as the

[40] Bugnini, p. 661.

General Instruction of the Roman Missal. The group thus took a part in the overall renewal of the 1614 Roman Ritual, specifically of Title V on the Most Blessed Sacrament of the Eucharist, which contained a range of topics after its general introduction: the order of administering Holy Communion, juridic-pastoral norms on Easter communion, the rite of communion of the sick, instructions concerning a priest celebrating Mass twice on the same day, and instructions concerning a priest who is blind. The group also treated more recent norms on exposing the Most Blessed Sacrament, especially on the solemnity of the Most Holy Body and Blood of Christ. "In no way therefore should anyone seek in these pages of the directory anything complete and systematic under the doctrinal, pastoral and ritual aspect, concerning all the things that have a connection to worship of the eucharistic mystery."[41] However, the group did prepare for the document a new ritual part and a pastoral-normative part.

The new outline from this work grew from matters raised at the end of EM and remains the basic outline of the finished ritual book. After a general introduction, the schema presented its topics in three chapters. The first was the order of administering Holy Communion outside Mass with its own introduction. This contained one form joined to a celebration of the Word of God, as well as a brief form.

The second chapter presented different forms of worship toward the Most Blessed Sacrament. It too carried its own introduction before presenting the nature of exposition of the Most Holy Eucharist, and then the order of exposition of the Most Blessed Sacrament with its parts: exposition, adoration, Benediction, and reposition of the Most Blessed Sacrament. It then treated eucharistic processions and eucharistic congresses.

The third chapter collected different texts: Scripture readings, hymns, antiphons, responsories, versicles, prayers after

[41] Schema 403, p. 1.

communion, and prayers for Benediction of the Most Blessed Sacrament.

The Congregation for Divine Worship reviewed the group's work at its plenary meeting a few weeks later on March 7, 1972.[42] This led to the last of the schemata in hand, number 405, from April 20. It followed the same outline as its predecessor and made relatively few changes. Early the following year, the congregation sent the work to the Congregations for the Doctrine of the Faith, of the Sacraments, and of Religious for their review. The Congregation for Divine Worship published the final liturgical book on the solemnity of the Most Holy Body and Blood of Christ, June 21, 1973.[43] The first English translation was published in 1976.[44]

The Revised Translation and Publication

The International Commission on English in the Liturgy worked on a revised translation of the book from about 2018 to 2020. The original translation had been quite faithful to the typical edition, so it did not require many changes. Still, the revision coheres in style with other work the commission had accomplished in previous years and under revised guidelines governing liturgical translation.

Such a project begins with a base translator, who submits work to the ICEL secretariat in Washington, DC. ICEL's editorial committee, which has experience with previous translations, reviews and revises the submission for style and content. For this project, those steps had been completed by 2018, but the commission of bishops representing ICEL's eleven conferences was unable to review it until early 2020 due to other items crowding their annual agenda. Then, having addressed issues

[42] Bugnini, p. 662, citing Notitiae 8 (1972), pp. 120–22, http://www.cultodivino.va/content/cultodivino/it/rivista-notitiae/indici-annate/1972/72.html.

[43] Bugnini, pp. 662–63.

[44] *Holy Communion and Worship of the Eucharist outside Mass* (New York: Catholic Book Publishing Co., 1976).

ranging from the theological to the grammatical, the commission sent the work to their conferences for review. This "green book" prompted the conferences to tender suggestions to improve the translation. The commission of bishops reconvened to review these before sending the "gray book" back to the conferences, drawing ICEL's work on this project to its conclusion.

Any conference wishing to change the gray book contacts the Vatican's Dicastery for Divine Worship and Discipline of the Sacraments. After its review, the dicastery sends its approved translation back to the conference. The USCCB proposed several emendations based on local traditions and its own supplemental publication that had already addressed some concerns of the first translation.

In 1993, the bishops of the United States published an auxiliary book for exposition of the Blessed Sacrament.[45] The 1973 typical edition from the Vatican contains the order of service for Benediction, while allowing some flexibility in the celebration. However, its few pages seemed more an explanation of the ritual than a service book. In reality, not every parish owned a copy of the 1976 translation, many priests seemed unaware of it, and services of Benediction took place using other traditional aids. In an effort to establish uniformity of practice and a helpful guide, the bishops' committee on the liturgy had compiled its own book to assist, which they described as "a collection of rites and texts for use during the Solemn Exposition of the Holy Eucharist."[46]

When the USCCB reviewed the revised English translation, its members saw that it did not address some of the issues it resolved in 1993 that they hoped to reuse for the practice in the conference. For example, they wished to set within the order of service the complete texts of the traditional hymns *O salutaris hostia* and *Tantum ergo*, both in Latin and in English. The Holy See had already approved ICEL's translation of these within

[45] *Order for the Solemn Exposition of the Holy Eucharist: Presider's Edition* (Collegeville, MN: Liturgical Press, 1993).

[46] *Order for Solemn Exposition*, p. vi.

the sweeping project of hundreds of hymns from the Liturgy of the Hours, and they already existed in a separate chapter. The presence of these two eucharistic hymns within the order of service would not exclude the option of using others, but it would encourage the traditional practice in the United States and foster a more unified celebration nationwide. The Holy See granted the bishops' request.

During exposition of the Blessed Sacrament, after the *Tantum ergo*, it has been customary in the United States to add the verse and response *Panem de cælo*. Even though these have not appeared in the ritual book since its debut in 1973, many generations of Catholics in the United States knew them in both Latin and English, and sang them during adoration. Without an official English translation, variations persisted. The bishops hoped to make one version uniform. This request was not granted, perhaps to retain the original vision of this revised liturgy. As the revisions had removed the dialogue from communion outside Mass, so it was removed here.

Customarily, exposition has concluded with the Divine Praises. These too were not included in the typical edition, but the bishops of the United States wanted to add them as an option. This would similarly lead to a more consistent translation in practice. Their request was granted. A common translation of the Divine Praises may now be used at the end of the period of adoration and before reposition of the Blessed Sacrament.

The USCCB sought other changes. A priest or deacon commonly wears a cope for exposition, but the typical edition mentions it only for the sake of giving the blessing with the Blessed Sacrament. The rubrics would clarify that the ordained minister could wear the cope from the beginning of the service. This clarification was granted.

The bishops noted that the typical edition suggests celebrating part of the Liturgy of the Hours in conjunction with a period of exposition. However, it gives no rubrics for it, especially relevant to the blessing that concludes Morning and Evening Prayer. They proposed helpful guidance, such as omitting the blessing within the Liturgy of Hours, in favor of anticipating benediction with the Blessed Sacrament. The inclusion of this guidance has been approved. If Morning or Evening Prayer takes place within a period of adoration, it concludes with the text beginning, "May the Lord bless us," as in private recitation of those hours, or when a layperson presides. But if Morning or Evening Prayer concludes the period of adoration, even those words are omitted and Benediction with the Blessed Sacrament follows immediately.

During Benediction in the United States, as the deacon or priest holding the monstrance imparts a blessing over the people, another minister commonly incenses the Blessed Sacrament. The rubrics in the typical edition did not call for this. Even the preceding Roman Ritual made no mention of incense during the blessing. The practice may have evolved from the rubrics of the Mass, which permit incensation during the consecration as the priest shows the host and the chalice to the people. Nonetheless, because of the widespread practice, the bishops suggested adding incense during the blessing as an option. The ritual's omission of incense at this moment may have deliberately signaled that the time of adoration had yielded to a time of blessing. Nevertheless, the incensation during the blessing has been approved as an option.

After the blessing, English-speaking churches in the United States customarily add the hymn "Holy God, We Praise Thy Name." The ritual book allows an acclamation, but the bishops proposed the option of singing this popular hymn. Permission was granted for singing any hymn as an alternative to an acclamation.

All these proposed changes pertained to the second half of the typical edition, worship of the eucharistic mystery. The first half, concerning the distribution of Holy Communion outside Mass, received no objections or suggestions from the conference.[47]

[47] These paragraphs draw from internal communications of the USCCB's Committee on Divine Worship.

The revised title of the work similarly remains without comment. Previously in English, the typical edition has been called *Holy Communion and Worship of the Eucharist outside Mass*. Now it bears the title *Holy Communion and Worship of the Eucharistic Mystery outside Mass*. The people are receiving and worshiping the mystery that the Eucharist represents.

In the drafts, the work held two other titles. The first, *Sacramental Communion and Eucharistic Worship outside Mass*,[48] perhaps fell out of favor because "sacramental communion" does not sufficiently distinguish the celebration of the sacrament during Mass and the reception of its fruits outside Mass, and because "eucharistic worship" could sound like a characteristic of worship, rather than the object of worship. The second title, *Most Blessed Eucharist or Holy Communion and Worship of the Eucharist outside Mass*,[49] is closer to the one that remains. The first words recall the title of the relevant section from the 1614 Roman Ritual, "The Most Blessed Sacrament of the Eucharist," but these words also describe the Mass, which is not the subject of this series of rituals.

In the title that remains, now more fully translated into English, the word "Eucharist" has been changed to "Eucharistic Mystery," reflecting the expression that had always been there since the Latin typical edition. "Eucharist" can refer to the Mass or to Holy Communion within Mass. "Eucharistic Mystery" clarifies that this book concerns what takes place outside Mass. It also recalls the Vatican's 1967 instruction of the same title, which so thoroughly imbued the work that led to this liturgical book.

[48] Schema 401, p. 1.

[49] Schema 403, p. 6; and Schema 405, p. 6 (*sic*, but the second page of this particular schema).

General Introduction

Spanning both theory and praxis, the general introduction of HC surveys four areas. Its first two sections cover the relationship between eucharistic worship and the Mass, as well as the purpose of reserving the Eucharist. It then treats the place of eucharistic reservation and covers matters pertaining to the conference of bishops. This introduction relies on the work that Carlo Braga had accomplished after the study group set aside the one from the early draft in favor of a synthesis of documents already available.

The introduction first declares the centrality of the celebration of the Eucharist (HC 1), a theme that recurs throughout the volume. HC specifically deals with what is not Mass, but it cannot do so effectively without first establishing the place of Mass. To that end, the first paragraph offers a generous quote from the Second Vatican Council's decree *Presbyterorum Ordinis* on the ministry and life of priests, which addresses not only the Eucharist but also its relationship to other liturgical acts. The drafts opened with the same quote, but citing *Eucharisticum Mysterium* 6, which in turn was citing *Presbyterorum Ordinis* 5.[1]

The introduction cites EM 3e to show that the Mass is the origin and purpose of worship, the celebration in which Christ begins to be present in the sacrament. Then referring to *Mysterium Fidei*, it calls for the fitting reservation of this eucharistic presence in churches and oratories (HC 2). The late drafts

[1] Schema 403 (1), p. 6; and Schema 405 (1), p. 6.

referred here to EM 3b, which in turn cited *Mysterium Fidei*.[2] As in the first paragraph, the final version of the introduction gives the original source.

Because of this enduring presence of Christ, worship is due to the eucharistic species even outside Mass (HC 3). This paragraph relies on EM 3f, which in turn cites teaching from the Council of Trent. It comes from the late drafts.[3]

Correct devotion to the Eucharist therefore comes from both the celebration of the Mass and worship of the reserved sacrament (HC 4). This point comes from EM 3g and the late drafts.[4]

The second section of the introduction concerns the purpose of reserving the Eucharist (HC 5), relying on EM 49, as cited in the late drafts.[5] Showing one example of why schema 401 needed revision, it erroneously cited EM 55 when it declared, "The purpose of reserving the Eucharist is also in this, that the faithful are enticed toward sacramental or spiritual communion and are disposed toward it."[6]

Surprising to many Catholics is the declaration that the principal and original purpose of reserving the Eucharist is for Viaticum, or communion to the dying. Not only do many Catholics presume that the principal purposes of reservation are the secondary ones noted in this number (the distribution of communion and adoration of the Blessed Sacrament), but many do not realize that they are expected to receive Viaticum while they are still conscious enough to speak and swallow, and when death is near.

Christ is present in various modes: in the assembly, in the proclamation of the Scriptures, in the minister, and above all in the eucharistic species. Although uncited here, this belief

[2] Schema 403 (2), p. 6; and Schema 405 (2), p. 6.
[3] Schema 403 (3), p. 7; and Schema 405 (3), p. 7.
[4] Schema 403 (4), p. 7; and Schema 405 (4), p. 7.
[5] Schema 403 (5), p. 7; and Schema 405 (5), p. 7.
[6] Schema 403 (128), p. 34.

had already appeared in the Constitution on the Sacred Liturgy (SC 7) and in EM 9. In *Mysterium Fidei,* Paul VI called this last mode the presence par excellence, a point that the drafts had not made.[7] Because of this belief, Mass is not celebrated on an altar with a tabernacle where the species are already reserved. The real presence of Christ in the Eucharist is the fruit of the Mass (HC 6). This teaching changed the location of tabernacles in nearly every Catholic church in the world.[8] The Vatican's Secretariat of State assisted in the formulation of this number and successfully avoided further disputes on the relative presences of Christ.[9]

A sufficient number of consecrated hosts is to be kept for communion of the sick and for others outside Mass. These should be frequently replaced to avoid spoiling, and they are kept in a pyx or other vessel (HC 7), probably meaning a ciborium, a rounded metal container with a lid. This number cites GIRM 323 and 329, yet even the Roman Ritual had made a similar point.[10] The late drafts permitted here regional variations in the kinds of metals for these vessels, but this had already entered GIRM 332.[11] An early draft presumed that the Blood of Christ might be reserved in tabernacles, and that care should be taken lest it spoil and need to be poured out.[12] This view did not advance into HC. It is never permitted to throw out the sacred species (canon 1367), and the Precious Blood is to be consumed at the end of Mass (GIRM 163, 182).

Churches are to remain open at hours convenient for the faithful to worship the sacrament (HC 8). The introduction

[7] Schema 403 (10), p. 8; and Schema 405 (10), p. 8. The final version repositioned this as number 6.

[8] *Rituale Romanum,* Titulus V, Caput I:7, p. 151.

[9] Bugnini, p. 662, n. 77, where he cites GIRM 7, but clearly means SC 7.

[10] *Rituale Romanum,* Titulus V, Caput I:6, p. 151.

[11] Schema 401 included more material from the GIRM, which has been removed (124–25), pp. 33–34. Schema 403 (12), p. 8; and Schema 405 (12), p. 8.

[12] Schema 401 (121), p. 33.

cites EM 51, which had requested several hours of open accessibility in the morning and in the evening. Canon 937 urges the same, though it admits there may be a grave reason to the contrary. Sadly, churches in the United States are targets for crimes, especially in cities, and the lack of security makes it dangerous to leave them open unattended for hours each day. The drafts had included the same notice a few paragraphs earlier, but here it makes a fitting transition to the next section.[13]

The introduction devotes several numbers to the place of reservation. The area should be prominent yet suited for private prayer, preferably in a separate chapel, especially inside churches often used for weddings and funerals, or frequented by visitors (HC 9). The drafts had requested the same, citing EM 53, a reference that the final version assigns to HC 10.[14] The tabernacle location pertains more to private prayer than to the celebration of the Eucharist. For this reason, many church renovations after the council moved the tabernacle off the center axis of the church, lending more precision to the purposes of the tabernacle and the altar.

The tabernacle is to be irremovable, solid, not transparent, and locked with a key kept hidden. Ordinarily there should be only one tabernacle in a church (HC 10). These prescriptions keep the most sacred part of the church secure, even when the building is open, and preserve the sacrament from the danger of profanation. Similar instructions had appeared in the previous Roman Ritual, when the tabernacle rested upon the principal altar.[15]

An early draft permitted episcopal conferences to approve tabernacles made of glass or crystal for the viewing of the vessel or the eucharistic species. "Nevertheless, a tabernacle

[13] Schema 403 (6), p. 7; and Schema 405 (6), p. 7.

[14] Schema 401 (129), p. 35; Schema 403 (8), p. 7; and Schema 405 (8), p. 7.

[15] *Rituale Romanum*, Titulus V, Caput I:6, p. 151.

in this case should ordinarily be covered with a canopy or curtain, perhaps needing to be removed when adoration of the sacrament has to take place."[16] That permission never entered the final version of HC. Glass tabernacles would create permanent exposition, which the introduction wishes to avoid. This number relies on EM 52 and 53, as well as 54, which is uncited, and canon 938. The drafts covered the same material, though in a different sequence.[17]

The drafts retained a notice from EM 54 that permitted the priest to celebrate Mass facing the people when he stood at an altar furnished with a tabernacle, as long as it was small yet adequate, citing *Inter Œcumenici* 95.[18] This permission was removed from the final version of HC because it no longer cohered with other legislation in force.

The introduction recommended indicating the presence of the sacrament by covering the tabernacle with a veil or using some other method. It also requested a special oil lamp or wax candle to honor the presence of Christ (HC 11). The Roman Ritual had made similar requirements.[19] The new rules derive from EM 57 and canon 940, and they appeared in the drafts.[20] One draft permitted a variety of additional options: distinctive lighting for the chapel, a canopy, a cloth specially woven and suspended in a fitting place, or even a banner on occasion.[21]

Finally, the introduction assigns to the conferences of bishops authority over local popular traditions, translations, and music (HC 12). This was missing from the drafts, but it matches the concerns of the final section of the introduction in other liturgical books.

[16] Schema 401 (128), p. 34.
[17] Schema 403 (7), p. 7; and Schema 405 (7 and 9), pp. 7–8.
[18] Schema 403 (9), p. 8; and Schema 405 (10), p. 8.
[19] *Rituale Romanum*, Titulus V, Caput I:7, p. 151.
[20] Schema 403 (11), p. 8; and Schema 405 (11), p. 8.
[21] Schema 401 (132), p. 35.

Holy Communion outside Mass

The next chapters of HC pertain to the liturgies described in the title: the reception of Holy Communion outside Mass and the forms of worship of the Most Blessed Sacrament. Each carries its own introduction.

In the first instance, the introduction stands at the head of a section concerning the ordinary administration of communion outside Mass. A second chapter, presuming the same introduction, addresses specific concerns pertaining to the sick and the dying.

Introduction

The introduction considers several topics: the relation between communion within Mass and outside it, the time for communion outside Mass, the minister, the location, norms for distributing communion, and the proper dispositions for those who wish to receive.

The first section deals with the important theological distinction between receiving communion at Mass and receiving communion outside Mass. The more perfect of the two ways to receive is within Mass, and its meaning is clearer when the people receive communion after the priest from bread and wine consecrated at the same Mass, preferably from recently baked bread (HC 13). The Constitution on the Sacred Liturgy similarly called for the people to receive communion from elements consecrated at the same Mass (SC 55). GIRM 85 also favors the practice. The drafts noted the same points from EM 31 and

33a.[1] HC 13 recalls number 1, which introduced its treatment of the eucharistic mystery outside Mass by throwing the spotlight onto Mass. It foreshadows numbers 14, 80, and 82.

This requested a significant change from the previous practice. The Roman Ritual had urged pastors to encourage the communion of the people frequently, "especially on the major solemnities of the year."[2] Without reference to their participation in the eucharistic sacrifice, the ritual asked the faithful to approach communion in humility, having fasted and confessed serious sin, kneeling in adoration, and with the men preferably separated from the women.[3] The faithful sometimes received communion either before or after Mass in a separate, brief liturgical ritual beginning with the *Confiteor*. The practice began in the ninth century to accommodate the large number of people seeking communion on certain feasts, but it remained common even when those numbers diminished.[4] HC permits communion outside Mass, but not without stressing the preferred way of receiving communion during Mass.

The preference for bread recently baked appears also in the missal (GIRM 320). Although this is not much practiced, providing freshly baked bread for the Eucharist strengthens the sense of immediacy, enhances flavor, fosters sharing a common loaf, discourages reserving unnecessarily large quantities, and builds the kind of community evident whenever people share a meal.

Although the faithful are to receive communion during Mass, they may seek it outside Mass for a just cause. Reasons may include communion to the sick, the aged, and those in danger of death, which connects them to the eucharistic sacri-

[1] Schema 401 (14), p. 6; Schema 403 (1), p. 9; and Schema 405 (1), p. 9.

[2] *Rituale Romanum*, Titulus V, Caput I:2, p. 150.

[3] *Rituale Romanum*, Titulus V, Caput I:3, p. 150.

[4] Robert Cabié and others, *The Church at Prayer: An Introduction to the Liturgy*, ed. Aimé Georges Martimort, vol. 3, *The Sacraments*, trans. Matthew J. O'Connell (Collegeville, MN: Liturgical Press, 1988), p. 42.

fice and to the community of people who know and love them. The sick may even receive under the form of wine alone, as indicated in EM 41 (HC 14). Unmentioned among the causes is the shortage or unavailability of priests, without whom another minister may offer communion to those deprived of Mass.

The late drafts also encouraged priests to provide communion outside Mass, especially to the sick.[5] As the published version ultimately did, these also cited EM 33a and 40. These drafts and HC 14 make a laudable appeal for providing communion especially during Easter Time, when the Church celebrates the resurrection of Christ, who is present in the eucharistic species. However, in practice, few parishes make a special effort to increase ministry to the sick during those seven weeks of the liturgical year.

HC 15 stresses again that communion outside Mass still connects one to the Mass and with those who participate in the sacred banquet, citing EM 3a. The drafts made the same point.[6]

Next the introduction widened the time for administering Holy Communion outside Mass. This may now be done on any day and at any time of day, at the convenience of the faithful, so that they may obtain the greatest spiritual benefit. Exceptions exist during the paschal Triduum: on Holy Thursday and Good Friday, only the sick may receive outside the main services, and on Holy Saturday communion may only be administered as Viaticum to the dying (HC 16).

Regarding the time of day, because the Roman Ritual had required fasting from midnight,[7] communion outside Mass generally took place in the early hours of the morning. Indeed, it required distribution only at the times when Mass was able

[5] Schema 403 (2), p. 9; and Schema 405 (2), p. 9.

[6] Schema 403 (3), p. 9; and Schema 405 (3), p. 9.

[7] *Rituale Romanum*, Titulus V, Caput I:2, p. 150.

to be offered, outside a grave cause.[8] Now with the reduced requirements for fasting, the faithful may more easily receive communion at any hour.

The Roman Ritual had set different rules for the paschal Triduum. It made no changes to Holy Thursday, so the faithful could have received communion before the Mass of the Lord's Supper, even if they were not sick. Communion apart from the main service on Good Friday had been restricted to Viaticum. The service now known as the Easter Vigil took place earlier in the day on Holy Saturday, so communion could have been distributed to the faithful during it or after it. Viaticum was always available at any day or hour.[9]

The new rules came from the postconciliar Roman Missal. They also appeared in the late drafts.[10] An early draft nonetheless pleaded for avoiding the excessive repetition of distributing communion outside Mass on any particular day.[11]

The third section of the introduction deals with the minister (HC 17). The priest or deacon should devote time to this ministry, as EM 31 had stated. An instituted acolyte may replace an ordained minister unable to perform the duty, or may assist when the number of communicants at Mass is great, as Paul VI had established in *Ministeria Quædam*. The local ordinary may give the faculty of distributing communion to other extraordinary ministers, as the Congregation for the Discipline of the Sacraments had established in its instruction *Immensæ Caritatis* (1, I and II).

The approval of individuals to serve as extraordinary lay ministers of Holy Communion belongs to the ordinary, more so than the approval of other ministers such as a reader, usher, or server. The ordinary oversees communion ministry more

[8] *Rituale Romanum*, Titulus V, Caput I:17, p. 153.
[9] *Rituale Romanum*, Titulus V, Caput I:17, p. 153.
[10] Schema 403 (4), p. 9; and Schema 405 (4), p. 9.
[11] Schema 401 (21), p. 8.

carefully, probably due to its key connection to the Eucharist and to the Church's desire to improve accessibility to the sacrament. In practice, he often delegates the approval to priests.

Before the council, only a priest was the ordinary minister of Holy Communion. A deacon was considered an extraordinary minister, exercising the role with permission of the ordinary or the pastor in a case of legitimate necessity.[12] The pastor was especially charged with bringing communion to the sick, though other priests could do it out of necessity with at least the presumed permission of the pastor.[13] A deacon bringing communion to the sick used the same rite as the priest.[14]

The drafts at first acknowledged that the ordinary could appoint one of the following individuals in the absence of a priest or deacon: an acolyte or another cleric (*sic;* acolytes were no longer considered clerics); a man in religious life, a monk, or a religious sister, if judged necessary; and, finally, even a layman or a laywoman.[15] That hierarchy of candidates originally appeared in the instruction *Fidei Custos* (3). The list disappeared from a later draft and remains absent from HC.[16]

The fourth section of the introduction concerns the place for distributing communion. A church or oratory makes an ideal location, but a minister may bring Holy Communion to other places, including homes, hospitals, and prisons (HC 18). The drafts covered the same permissions.[17]

Norms for the distribution of communion appear in the fifth section. At church, the altar is covered with a cloth and a corporal, and two candles are lighted as a sign of veneration and of a banquet, citing GIRM 307. Outside a church, a suitable table is to be covered with a cloth; candles are optional (HC

[12] *Rituale Romanum,* Titulus V, Caput I:13, p. 152.

[13] *Rituale Romanum,* Titulus V, Caput IV:7, p. 161.

[14] *Rituale Romanum,* Titulus V, Caput IV:29, p. 168.

[15] Schema 401 (18), p. 7; and Schema 403 (5), p. 10.

[16] Schema 405 (5), p. 10.

[17] Schema 401 (19), p. 7; Schema 403 (6), p. 10; and Schema 405 (6), p. 10.

19). Indeed, in prisons and hospitals, for example, lighting candles would not likely be permitted.

A corporal is rarely used outside the celebration of Mass. It usually appears on the altar as part of the preparation of the gifts to designate the area for the sacrifice and consecration of the bread and wine. The use of one here retains a practice from the preconciliar rubrics, where the priest placed a corporal on the altar in front of the tabernacle before removing the ciborium. In fact, upon entering the sanctuary, he was allowed to process toward the altar carrying the burse containing the corporal; candles were to be lighted.[18] (The burse is not mentioned in HC nor anywhere in the missal.) Also, according to the preconciliar rubrics, when a minister brought communion to the sick, a nearby table was to be covered with a clean linen cloth, not specified to be a corporal, which was less accessible outside a church.[19] Lighted candles were to be provided.[20]

The 1969 private draft of the rite for administering Holy Communion had called for lighted candles and a corporal (1). The same directives appeared in the other drafts, though they did not mention the devotional and festal purpose of the candles as HC 18 does.[21]

For vesture today, a priest or deacon wears a stole over an alb or over a cassock and surplice. Lay ministers wear either the vesture traditional in their region or whatever has been approved by the ordinary. Outside a church, the Eucharist is to be carried in a pyx or another closed vessel, covered in an appropriate way (HC 20). Some ministers place the pyx inside a small cloth burse that hangs by a string around the neck, though the rubrics do not require this. In the United States, GIRM 339 describes the vesture for lay ministers at Mass as

[18] *Rituale Romanum*, Titulus V, Caput II:1, p. 154.
[19] *Rituale Romanum*, Titulus V, Caput IV:10, p. 162.
[20] *Rituale Romanum*, Titulus V, Caput IV:11, p. 162.
[21] Schema 401 (23), p. 8; Schema 403 (7), p. 10; and Schema 405 (7), p. 10.

the alb or other appropriate and dignified clothing. Something similar would logically apply here.

In the Roman Ritual, the priest wore a surplice and stole over his cassock to distribute communion at church.[22] However, if he distributed communion before or after a private Mass, which was also common, he wore the chasuble.[23] This provided some convenience for the priest at the time, but it no longer applies. He wears a chasuble only for Mass and for the celebration of the Passion on Good Friday.

In the same Roman Ritual, when bringing communion to the sick, the priest was first to enclose the host in a vessel covered with a clean veil, holding it with reverence and fear, and walking behind a server carrying a candle.[24] He rang the church bells to summon parishioners to join him in the procession.[25] Wearing surplice and stole, or even a cope, he put on the humeral veil, held the receptacle before him, and walked without wearing a hat but beneath a canopy or umbrella.[26] When riding on horseback, he took extra care to fasten the vessel around his neck.[27]

The 1969 private draft of the ritual simplified all of this, calling for the minister to vest appropriate to the sacred mystery, without mentioning how (2). The remaining drafts asked a cleric to dress in alb or surplice, and a deacon or priest to wear a stole.[28] Outside a church, a cleric would laudably dress the same way.[29] Those who were not clerics wore clothing that was completely appropriate to the ministry.[30]

[22] *Rituale Romanum*, Titulus V, Caput II:1, p. 154.
[23] *Rituale Romanum*, Titulus V, Caput II:13, p. 158.
[24] *Rituale Romanum*, Titulus V, Caput IV:6, p. 161.
[25] *Rituale Romanum*, Titulus V, Caput IV:10, p. 162.
[26] *Rituale Romanum*, Titulus V, Caput IV:12, pp. 162–163.
[27] *Rituale Romanum*, Titulus V, Caput IV:13, p. 163.
[28] Schema 401 (23), p. 8.
[29] Schema 401 (24), p. 8.
[30] Schema 403 (8), p. 10. Oddly, number 8 is missing from schema 405.

In an early draft, to carry the vessel from the tabernacle to the altar, a cleric was to wear an alb or surplice, and a priest or deacon wore a stole as well. Candles were to be used. However, when carrying the Eucharist outside the church, no special vesture was required. The host was to be carried in a pyx or small vessel, taking great care that it closed securely. It was appropriate to place it in a cloth burse attached to strings that one could drape around one's neck.[31] These directives were quickly simplified further: "In carrying the sacred Eucharist for administering communion outside the church, the sacred species should be carried enclosed in a pyx or another vessel, with vesture and manner appropriate according to the customs of places."[32]

Distributing communion on the tongue of the faithful is retained as a time-honored custom, but conferences of bishops, with approval of the Apostolic See, may allow a minister to place the consecrated host in the hand of the communicant. As noted in *Immensæ Caritatis* (4), the faithful should be taught about the divinity of Christ, and that his presence in the Eucharist deserves the same adoration due to God. As in OM 134 and GIRM 286, in distributing communion, the minister says, "The Body of Christ" (or: "The Blood of Christ"), and the communicant answers "Amen" (HC 21).[33] The Vatican's Secretariat of State, implementing comments of Paul VI, intervened in wording this number, probably because it concerned the manner of receiving communion.[34]

The minister is to collect remaining fragments and place them in a pyx or rinse them in a vessel with water. A vessel used for the Blood of Christ should be washed with water. The

[31] Schema 401 (22), p. 8.

[32] Schema 403 (9), p. 11; and Schema 405 (9), p. 11.

[33] The typical edition cites GIRM 242, which has become 283 in the third edition of the Roman Missal, but 244d, which is now 286, is more pertinent to the topic of this number.

[34] Bugnini, p. 662, fn. 77.

water is to be drunk or poured out in an appropriate place (HC 22), which most likely means the sacrarium, if available, and, if not, some other place where the water goes directly into the ground.

In the Roman Ritual, the priest had used both water and wine for the ablution of the vessels, even outside Mass.[35] Any remaining water was to be poured down the sacrarium or, in the absence of a sacrarium, thrown into fire.[36]

HC 22 does not limit this action to any rank of minister, so even a lay minister is expected to cleanse the vessels in this way. The same applies to the minister of communion to the sick (55). The rubrics of the Mass mention only an ordained minister or instituted acolyte performing a similar action (GIRM 192, 279). The missal calls this action a "purification" at Mass, and HC 22 calls it an "ablution" outside Mass. Nonetheless, cleansing the vessel is part of a lay minister's competency when administering communion outside Mass. As will be seen, "purification" is the word used in Latin and in English for cleansing the vessel after administering communion to the sick (HC 62).

In the drafts, after distributing communion in a church, the minister was to wipe the ciborium with a cloth to push the fragments into another vessel, as indicated in what is now GIRM 279. Outside a church, the minister was to put a little water in the empty vessel to consume what remains of the fragments, or to dispose of the water in an appropriate place. If a chalice or other vessel was used for the Blood of Christ, it too was to be "purified,"[37] a word that HC removed.

The final section of the introduction deals with the dispositions for receiving communion. The Eucharist is the fount of

[35] *Rituale Romanum*, Titulus V, Caput II:1, p. 154.

[36] *Rituale Romanum*, Titulus V, Caput II:8, p. 157.

[37] Schema 401 (25), p. 9. See also Schema 403 (10), p. 11; and Schema 405 (10), p. 11.

all grace, but communicants are to come with clean consciences. Those in mortal sin unable to confess first, perhaps due to the inaccessibility of priests in their region, should receive after making a perfect act of contrition, and then present themselves for confession when a priest next becomes available. Daily communicants are to celebrate reconciliation at regular intervals. As EM 35 notes, all should use the penitential parts of the liturgy to assist in overcoming faults (HC 23).

"Perfect contrition" is an expression found in EM 35 and canon 916, both of which echo this point. Perfect contrition is a disposition in which one's remorse for sin comes from one's love of God, rather than one's fear of punishment. The drafts treated this material in a similar way.[38]

Expecting the faithful to use the penitential parts of the Mass may have two purposes. One may simply be to extract the most benefit from participation, acknowledging one's sins especially in the penitential act of the introductory rites. Indeed, the faithful also express contrition in the Gloria and the Lamb of God, which appeal for the mercy of Christ, who takes away the sins of the world. Additionally, when the deacon or priest kisses the book at the conclusion of the gospel, he prays that sins may be wiped away. Furthermore, the priest prays for the cleansing of his sins at the washing of his hands.

Alternatively, the expectation to use the penitential elements of the liturgy may aim to distinguish between these parts of the Mass and the sacrament of reconciliation. God forgives sins in many ways, but this sacrament is unique and necessary for the forgiveness of mortal sin.

The introduction reminds communicants to fast an hour (HC 24), though it makes exceptions for the sick and elderly and even those caring for them, as noted in canon 919, sections 1 and 3. The drafts had made similar points.[39]

[38] Schema 403 (12), p. 11; and Schema 405 (12), p. 11.

[39] Schema 401 (28–29), p. 10; Schema 403 (11), p. 11; and Schema 405 (11), p. 11.

Under the Holy Spirit, the effects of Holy Communion should make an impact on one's daily life, producing acts of thanks and performing works of charity toward others (HC 25). Even outside Mass, spending some time in prayer immediately after communion will help a person extend thanks to God, as noted in EM 38.

One theme of the work of the Second Vatican Council was to underscore the role of the Holy Spirit in the Church. The reference to the Spirit in HC 25 shows one example of the fruit of this perspective. The drafts had presented similar ideas.[40]

The Order of Distributing Holy Communion outside Mass: The Rite with a Fuller Celebration of the Word of God

The minister chooses between two forms for distributing communion: with a fuller or a brief celebration of the Word of God. The preconciliar Roman Ritual effectively had two choices as well: communion outside Mass and communion within Mass using the rite for distributing communion outside Mass. The Mass included a celebration of the Word of God, but communion outside Mass did not. As with many other rituals of the preconciliar liturgy, readings from Sacred Scripture were absent. The Word of God is so central to the revised ritual that the two versions of its title both make reference to it, the only distinction being the amount of time devoted to Sacred Scripture.

The opening of this section explains this novel and central approach: the sacred Word reveals God's wonders, which reach their preeminence in the paschal mystery celebrated in the Mass. Communion shares in that mystery, and the Word of God leads the faithful to participate in it worthily (HC 26). A word service with communion may be used when Mass has not taken place or when the distribution of communion is

[40] Schema 401 (70), p. 18; Schema 403 (13), p. 11; and Schema 405 (13), p. 11.

established at certain times. On Sundays, including Saturday evening, a communion service may not be offered in the same church where Mass has taken place.[41] The same restriction does not apply to weekdays.

At first the drafts also distinguished two options, called simply the longer form and the brief form, without mentioning the Word of God. In fact, only the first of these included readings, which were among the elements excluded from the second form.[42] A later draft explained the distinction more fully, though the second form did include reading a verse from the Bible, which was still more than its predecessor offered.

> A rite with a twofold form is proposed: the first is indeed to be enacted with the celebration of the Word of God, according to the format used in Mass, and which may be appropriately used in those places where, especially on a Sunday, the Eucharist cannot be celebrated, or in churches where after or before a celebrated Mass, the distribution of communion takes place at a set hour and for the advantage of some group of the faithful, not of one or another individual. This conjunction of the Word of God with the sacrament responds to the norm of the restoration that the Constitution on the Sacred Liturgy manifests (art. 35, 1). The structure of the rite foresees above all a penitential act in the form used at the beginning of Mass, and also the communion rite that happens at Mass: the Lord's Prayer, the rite of peace (which is still "if appropriate"), and of course communion itself, and the conclusion with the blessing and dismissal.
>
> The other form of the rite, simpler and shorter, is proposed to be used when Holy Communion is given either

[41] Congregation for Divine Worship, "Directory for Sunday Celebrations in the Absence of a Priest," par. 21, *Sunday Celebrations in the Absence of a Priest* (Washington, DC: United States Conference of Catholic Bishops, 2012), p. 164.

[42] Schema 401 (31), p. 10; and (52), p. 13.

> to one or another or only a few individuals, but without the aforementioned celebration of the Word. It is still recommended that there take place at least a brief reading of one or another versicle that speaks of the bread of life, to make note of the connection between the word and sacrament. The other parts, with obvious simplifications that are necessary in this rite, repeat the format of the preceding form.[43]

Regarding the title, the drafts called the first version "Form Joined with a Celebration of the Word of God."[44] A few changes happened in the final version of HC. The word "form" changed to "rite" to cohere with other liturgical books: an entire book may be called an "order," but sections of it may be called "rites," as found, for example, within the order of Christian Initiation of Adults. The word for "joined," which remains in Latin atop HC 26, goes untranslated in English, probably because the word "with" implies it. The word "fuller," which the earliest draft used in the simplest of titles for this ritual, "Fuller Form,"[45] was removed from the subsequent drafts, but added to the final version. As a result, the ceremony is called a rite of the Church, and reading from the Word of God is implied no matter which of the two rites one chooses.

HC 26 explains the purpose of including the Word of God in this celebration where it had never been before. According to the late drafts,[46] this section relies on EM 10, which in turn cites the Second Vatican Council's Constitution on Divine Revelation, *Dei Verbum* (21). This liturgy reveres the Word of the Lord as well as the Body of the Lord, and offers a separate table for each.

[43] Schema 403, pp. 2–3.

[44] Schema 403, p. 12; and Schema 405, p. 12.

[45] Schema 401, p. 10.

[46] Schema 403 (14), p. 12; and Schema 405 (14), p. 12.

The Introductory Rites

Once the people have gathered, the minister greets them (HC 27). The preparation of the space and the vesture of the minister have already been treated in HC 19 and 20.

The gathering of the people seems obvious to mention, but those simple words resonate deeply. Prior to the postconciliar changes, the rubrics for the Order of Mass began with a reference to the priest: Mass began when he was vested and ready. But the first words in the revised Order of Mass are different: Mass begins after the people have gathered. The presence of the people signifies the centrality of their role in the celebration. It is not the priest's Mass, but the celebration of the Eucharist by the people of God.

Other ritual books describe the start of the ceremony in a similar way, such as the arrival of a single penitent to begin the sacrament of reconciliation in the Order of Penance (41). Even when receiving communion outside Mass, the gathering of the people precedes the start of the celebration.

The ritual does not mention the entrance of the minister. Perhaps the minister still enters from the sacristy or up the aisle, or perhaps the minister is present in the sanctuary as the people gather.

The ritual makes no reference to the use of the presider's chair. When a priest presides, he would obviously use it. A deacon arguably could use either the presider's chair or his own, but on Sundays in the United States he or another minister is not to use the presider's chair "as a symbol that the community awaits the presence of the Priest" (24).[47] The General Instruction on the Liturgy of the Hours says that a presider who is not a priest "is only one among equals and does not enter the sanctuary or greet and bless the people" (258). Here, however, a layperson needs to enter the sanctuary and does

[47] *Sunday Celebrations in the Absence of a Priest*, p. 14. See also no. 36, p. 16.

greet the people. Although one could argue that a layperson would therefore use the presider's chair, this liturgical book does not say so, and indications in other liturgical books suggest that one does not.

Nor is there an entrance antiphon as in the celebration of Mass or in a wedding without Mass (Order of Celebrating Matrimony 81). Consequently, the ritual does not even envision an opening hymn.

Nor does this ceremony begin with the sign of the cross. For many centuries this sign has opened the Mass, the ritual sacrament of the paschal mystery. However, distributing communion outside Mass requires that that celebration already have taken place.

The greeting changes depending on the minister (HC 27). As at Mass, if a priest or deacon greets the people, they respond, "And with your spirit." If the minister is a layperson, he or she greets the people with another formula, eliciting a different response. This sustains a long liturgical tradition that preserves one greeting and response for clergy. The options include only two of the three from the Order of Mass. HC places the missing greeting in its fourth chapter, which collects various texts that may be used throughout. There one finds a still familiar greeting with the two responses that the previous editions of the Roman Missal permitted: either "Blessed be the God and Father of our Lord Jesus Christ," or "And with your spirit" (HC 189). The third edition of the missal removed the first of these two responses, probably because it was so difficult to remember on the spot and to simplify the words of the people.

The greeting of a lay minister appeared in the early draft with a slight variation: "Bless the Lord, brothers and sisters, who invites you (us) to participate at his supper."[48] In later drafts this changed to "Bless the Lord, brothers and sisters, who invites you (us) to participate at the table of the Body of

[48] Schema 401 (32), p. 10.

Christ."[49] In the final version, the pronouns changed their order, "us" before "you," in the likelihood that the minister will be receiving communion together with the people. The destination of the invitation changed from the "supper" to the "table," probably to avoid any confusion between this celebration and the Eucharist. The Latin word for "in his goodness" was added to the final version, which also removed the Latin word for "participate," but the English translation inserts it with the word "share."

The rubrics then allow the minister to use other greetings from Scripture. A similar permission occurs in the Order of Celebrating Matrimony without Mass (86). However, the English translation there changed the permissible alternatives from greetings found in Scripture to greetings found in the Roman Missal.

The Penitential Act follows, as at Mass (HC 28). The rubric at Mass has the priest invite the faithful "to make the Penitential Act," but here the minister invites the communicants "to repentance."

The minister's spoken introduction differs slightly from the one at Mass and comes from the rites for anointing and giving pastoral care to the sick (PCS 118, or 52 and 233 in the Latin typical edition). At Mass the priest invites the faithful to prepare "to celebrate the sacred mysteries" (OM 4, 5 and 6), but here they are invited "to participate in this sacred celebration." The Mass is considered a celebration of the paschal mystery, but this service is different.

The drafts had proposed a different introduction, in these or similar words: "Brothers and sisters, let us acknowledge our sins, and so prepare ourselves to receive the Body of the Lord."[50] The revision clarifies that the reception of communion

[49] Schema 403 (15), p. 12; and Schema 405 (15), p. 12.

[50] Schema 401 (32), p. 11; Schema 403 (16), p. 13; and Schema 405 (16), p. 13.

is one part of a sacred celebration, the entirety of which deserves spiritual preparation.

Within the body of this order of service, the first option, the *Confiteor*, is given (HC 28). The other forms are in the fourth chapter (190–91). Although the missal seems to restrict the next of these options to the priest (OM 5), any lay minister may use it at a communion service (HC 190). The last of them lists three invocations that any one of those present may read (HC 191). The suggested invocations come from the rites for anointing and giving pastoral care to the sick (PCS 118, or 52 and 233 in the Latin typical edition), but other invocations may be composed or borrowed from the missal.

The 1969 private draft put the *Confiteor* or the act of contrition a bit later, after the Lord's Prayer (3). The location showed the influence of the Roman Ritual, which had the server recite the *Confiteor* after the priest's communion on behalf of the people who would soon also receive, even though the same general confession had already taken place earlier in the Mass.[51]

In the Roman Ritual, the priest then offered the words of absolution from the opening rites of the Mass, beginning with "May almighty God have mercy on you," instead of "on us," as was the custom at the time. The priest continued, "May the almighty and merciful Lord grant you pardon, absolution and remission of your sins," while making the sign of the cross over the people. The same two elements opened the Roman Ritual's five-part absolution in the sacrament of penance, though with the singular form of the pronoun "you."[52] Before distributing communion, the priest stopped there, without reciting the sacramental formula for the forgiveness of sins reserved for penance, which would have required an individual's confession of sins and a different liturgical setting.

[51] *Rituale Romanum*, Titulus V, Caput II:1, p. 154.
[52] *Rituale Romanum*, Titulus V, Caput II:1–2, pp. 154–155.

The 1969 draft carried the same principle forward. The people's repentance came not at the beginning of the service, but in the moments before their communion. HC 28 moved it to the start.

The Celebration of the Word of God

Readings are proclaimed as in the Liturgy of the Word at Mass. These may come from those assigned to the day or from the votive Masses of the Most Holy Eucharist or of the Most Precious Blood of Our Lord Jesus Christ. Other passages may be chosen, including those recommended for the votive Mass of the Most Sacred Heart of Jesus. One or more readings may be proclaimed, and a psalm or other song may be sung. Silence may be observed. The universal prayer concludes this fuller celebration of the Word (HC 29).

The Roman Ritual, as noted above, had no reading from Scripture within such a service outside Mass. The liturgical reform aimed to correct such omissions.

The 1969 private draft called for a "sacred celebration of the Word of God" when this service took place, especially on Sundays and holy days of obligation. It cited subsection 4 of SC 35 and *Inter Œcumenici* 37 to 39 for its foundation. It requested the same format as at Mass: the epistle and gospel assigned to the day, along with chants, especially those taken from the psalms. The minister would read a homily previously composed by the bishop or pastor. The universal prayer concluded the celebration of the Word (3).

The other drafts requested something similar, though without yet mentioning the votive Mass for the Most Sacred Heart of Jesus.[53] The earliest made a few specific suggestions about the Liturgy of the Hours that did not appear in the final version, but still offer helpful direction:

[53] Schema 403 (17), p. 14; and Schema 405 (17), p. 14.

> Some biblical reading takes place, which is fittingly taken from the Lectionary for Mass or the Liturgy of the Hours of the current day, especially on Sundays, solemnities, feasts and the important liturgical times.
>
> Responsorial songs among those also noted in the same books are also laudably used. A priest or a deacon may give the homily or make a pious exhortation. However, a lay person is allowed to read a homily written by the same ministers or another appropriate patristic text, for example from the Liturgy of the Hours, or to exhort those present in another way. It is equally suitable that a time of sacred silence or of meditation be observed.
>
> A prayer of intercession, which may also be taken from the missal or the Liturgy of the Hours, may take place.[54]

The late drafts collected their suggested biblical readings in the first section of the third chapter, "Diverse Texts." These came from the then pertinent numbers in the Lectionary for Mass for the votive Masses of the Most Holy Eucharist (904–9) and of the Most Precious Blood of Jesus (916–21). They also acknowledged that an appropriate short reading could be taken from among these.[55] These pertained not only to the distribution of Holy Communion outside Mass, but also to adoration and a procession of the Most Blessed Sacrament.

The final version of HC puts its various texts in chapter IV. The lectionary numbers for the votive Mass are indicated in chapter I (HC 29). Chapter IV lists each option for the votive Mass of the Most Holy Eucharist. In the Lectionary the New Testament readings appropriate for Easter Time are listed separately (Acts 2:42-47; Acts 10:34a, 37-43; Revelation 1:5-8; and Revelation 7:9-14), but these are integrated into chapter IV in biblical order. All of the readings recommended for the votive Mass of the Most Precious Blood of Jesus are a subset of the

[54] Schema 401 (34–36), p. 11.

[55] Schema 403, p. 30; and Schema 405, p. 30.

ones for the votive Mass of the Most Holy Eucharist. Even though the fourth chapter does not explain that, all the citations are there.

Similarly, all the references to readings in the Lectionary's votive Mass for the Sacred Heart of Jesus appear in chapter IV. The passages recommended for the weeks after Easter are integrated among the other New Testament readings. Ideally, during Easter Time, even in worship of the Eucharist outside Mass, the first readings would come from Acts or Revelation instead of the Old Testament, as happens at Mass and during other celebrations such as weddings and funerals.

The first edition of the Lectionary paired first readings and psalms for the votive Masses, just as it did for a typical Sunday or weekday. Although the second edition eliminated those connections, the sequence of readings formerly suggested still provides a helpful resource. These come from the votive Mass of the Most Holy Eucharist:

- Genesis 14:18-20 (HC 113) and verses from Psalm 110 (HC 134) connect passages about Melchizedek.
- Exodus 16:2-4, 12-15 (HC 115) and verses from Psalm 78 (HC 133) explore the significance of manna from heaven.
- Exodus 24:3-8 (HC 116) and verses from Psalm 116 with a refrain from 1 Corinthians 10 (HC 135) relate the blood of the old covenant with the chalice of Jesus's blood.
- Deuteronomy 8:2-3, 15b-16a (HC 117) and verses from Psalm 145 (HC 136) recall God's provident supply of food.
- 1 Kings 19:4-8 (HC 118) and verses from Psalm 78 (HC 133) relate Elijah's miraculous food for the journey with the Israelites' earlier gift of manna.
- Proverbs 9:1-6 (HC 119) and verses from Psalm 147 (HC 137) with a refrain from John 6 align Wisdom's invitation to eat and drink with God's gift of finest wheat and Jesus's invitation to eat his body and drink his blood.

- During Easter Time, Acts 2:42-47 (HC 120) and verses from Psalm 23 (HC 130) connect the apostolic community's breaking of bread with the Good Shepherd spreading a table.
- Acts 10:34a, 37-43 (HC 121) and verses from Psalm 34 (HC 131) recall meals the apostles took with Jesus, while inviting believers today to taste the goodness of the Lord.

Three New Testament readings stand alone (HC 122, 123, and 124). The gospels carry recommended versicles for the acclamation that precedes them:

- John 6:56 (HC 139) precedes Mark 14:12-16, 22-26 (HC 143), linking a line from the discourse on the Bread of Life with an account of the Last Supper.
- John 6:51 (HC 138) precedes Luke 9:11b-17 (HC 145) and connects another verse from the same discourse with an account of the miracle of the loaves.
- John 6:56 (HC 139) also precedes Luke 24:13-35 (HC 147), the post-resurrection appearance of Jesus at table on the road to Emmaus.
- John 6:57 (HC 140), from the discourse on the bread of life, precedes John 6:1-15 (HC 148), another account of the miracle of the loaves.
- John 6:51 (HC 138) also precedes John 6:24-35 (HC 149), the opening of the discourse on the Bread of Life.
- John 6:51 (HC 138) also precedes John 6:41-51 (HC 150), the heart of the same discourse.
- John 6:56 (HC 139) also precedes John 6:51-58 (HC 151), the climax of the same discourse.
- John 6:57 (HC 140) also precedes John 21:1-14 (HC 153), an appearance of Jesus after the resurrection when he gave bread to his followers.

From the votive Mass of the Most Precious Blood of Our Lord Jesus Christ, the first edition of the Lectionary offered these pairings:

- Exodus 12:21-27 (HC 114) and verses from Psalm 116 with a refrain from 1 Corinthians 10 (HC 135) connects the blood of the covenant with the offering of the Blood of Christ.
- Exodus 24:3-8 (HC 116) in this case precedes verses from Psalm 40 (HC 132) to connect the blood of the covenant with personal sacrifice, anticipating the self-offering of Jesus.
- During Easter Time, Revelation 1:5-8 (HC 128) with verses from Psalm 40 (HC 132) connects the Blood of Christ with a willing sacrifice.
- Revelation 7:9-14 (HC 129) joins with verses from Psalm 116 and a refrain from 1 Corinthians 10 (HC 135) to connect the Blood of the Lamb with the offering of the chalice of Christ's blood.

Several second readings stand alone (HC 124, 125, 126, and 127). The first edition of the Lectionary then recommended pairings of versicles with gospels:

- Revelation 1:5ab (HC 141) is the source behind the versicle recommended for Mark 14:12-16, 22-26 (HC 143), connecting testimony about the Blood of Christ with an account of the Last Supper.
- The same versicle also precedes Mark 15:16-20 (HC 144), where the soldiers mock Jesus and dress him in purple, the color of blood.
- Revelation 5:9 (HC 142) precedes Luke 22:39-44 (HC 146), proclaiming salvation by the Blood of Christ before hearing of his sweat pouring out like blood on the Mount of Olives.

- The same versicle also precedes John 19:31-37 (HC 152), where blood and water pours from the side of the crucified Christ.

For the votive Mass of the Most Sacred Heart of Jesus, the first edition of the Lectionary recommended additional pairings:

- Exodus 34:4b-7a, 8-9 (HC 154) and verses from Psalm 25 (HC 171) connect passages on the kindness and mercy of God.
- Deuteronomy 7:6-11 (HC 155) and verses from Psalm 33 (HC 172) portray God's love for the chosen people.
- Deuteronomy 10:12-22 (HC 156) and the same verses from Psalm 25 (HC 171) explore the covenant of God's love.
- Isaiah 49:13-15 (HC 157) and verses from Psalm 34 (HC 173) present God as a loving mother and provider of food.
- Jeremiah 31:1-4 (HC 158) and verses from Isaiah 12 (HC 169) reveal the everlasting font of God's love.
- Ezekiel 34:11-16 (HC 159) and verses from Psalm 23 (HC 170) rejoice in God's loving care as a shepherd.
- Hosea 11:1b, 3-4, 8c-9 (HC 160) and verses from Psalm 103 (HC 174) demonstrate the love of a forgiving God.
- During Easter Time, Revelation 3:14b, 20-22 (HC 167) and verses from Psalm 33 (HC 172) show the eagerness of God to nourish and dine with his people.
- Revelation 5:6-12 (HC 168) and verses from Psalm 103 (HC 174) celebrate those redeemed by the Blood of the Lamb, the source of mercy.

Several New Testament passages stand alone (HC 161, 162, 163, 164, 165, and 166). Again, the versicles are paired with gospels:

- Matthew 11:25 (HC 175) is the source for a versicle that comes from a gospel on the humility of the heart of Christ (HC 181).
- Matthew 11:29ab (HC 177) from the same gospel passage precedes Luke 15:1-10 (HC 182), concerning the rejoicing in heaven over a repentant sinner.
- Matthew 11:28 (HC 176), also from the same gospel, precedes Luke 15:1-3, 11-32 (HC 183), the parable of the prodigal son.
- John 10:14 (HC 178) comes from the gospel of the Good Shepherd, John 10:11-18 (HC 184).
- John 15:9 (HC 179) is the verse that follows John 15:1-8 (HC 185) on the love and unity between Jesus and his followers.
- The same versicle also precedes the gospel that includes it, John 15:9-17 (HC 186), where Jesus gives the command to mutual love.
- John 10:14 (HC 178) also precedes John 17:20-26, where Jesus prays for his followers, whom the Father loves (HC 187).
- 1 John 4:10b (HC 180) precedes John 19:31-37 (HC 188), showing the Father's love in sending the Son, from whose wounded side poured blood and water.

When using these passages today, one is not bound to these internal connections, but the first edition of the Lectionary offered some ways of combining passages so that the faithful may more deeply appreciate their meaning. They help explore the mystery of the Eucharist.

Holy Communion

The minister approaches the place of eucharistic reservation, removes the vessel containing previously consecrated hosts, places it on the altar, and genuflects. The minister introduces the Lord's Prayer (HC 30).

The rubrics call for only one genuflection. Upon opening a tabernacle door, the minister does not genuflect but carries the ciborium to the altar and genuflects there. This changes the practice from the preconciliar rubrics, where the priest genuflected upon removing the vessel from the tabernacle and then again before facing the people (without turning his back on the sacrament) for the absolution.[56] This coheres with the Council's aims to avoid needless repetitions and to concentrate meaning on each word and action.

An early draft put the genuflection at the tabernacle before bringing the ciborium to the altar.[57] The later drafts did not indicate any genuflection at all.[58] They simply instructed the minister to place the vessel on the altar and proceed with the Lord's Prayer. In the final version of HC, the minister genuflects at an appropriate time and place, when the people first see the vessel in front of them on the altar.

The Lord's Prayer begins the words of the communion rite (HC 30), just as at Mass, complete with the same introduction (OM 124), though the minister may use those or similar words. At Mass, in the presence of the newly consecrated Body and Blood of Christ, the Lord's Prayer best answers the unspoken question of the moment, "What could I possibly say now?" The community speaks the words that Jesus taught his disciples, allowing them to dare to call God the same title that Jesus used, while they beg for daily bread.

In the drafts, the instruction was similar. The 1969 private draft placed the Lord's Prayer after the universal prayer (3). An early draft instructed the minister to turn toward the people,[59] but the later drafts omitted this notice, perhaps

[56] *Rituale Romanum*, Titulus V, Caput II:1, 2 and 3, pp. 154–155.

[57] Schema 401 (37), p. 11.

[58] Schema 403 (18), p. 14; and Schema 405 (18), p. 14.

[59] Schema 401 (37), p. 11.

realizing that the minister would already be facing the people when setting the vessel on a freestanding altar. The minister was to introduce the Lord's Prayer with the formula from Mass or with another formula, and then all were to sing or recite the prayer together.[60] The same early draft omitted the complete text of the Lord's Prayer, which the others included.

As mentioned above, the 1969 private draft put the *Confiteor* after the Lord's Prayer. In it, the people omitted the direct address to the priest ("you, Father") that the server had included in the *Confiteor* at Mass before the reforms: "I confess to almighty God, to blessed Mary ever-virgin, blessed Michael the archangel, blessed John the Baptist, the holy apostles Peter and Paul, all the saints, and you, Father, that I have sinned . . ." Similarly, a few lines later the server had asked the same list of saints "and you, Father, to pray for me to the Lord our God." The same draft omitted that second reference to the priest as well. It permitted the people to replace the *Confiteor* with the act of contrition in force in their individual region.

As at Mass (OM 128), a sign of peace may be exchanged. According to the rubric, it retains the same purpose, an expression of peace and charity (HC 31). The 1969 private draft did not include this option. The others did, and the earliest of those supplied a different formula for use by a lay minister.[61] In Latin, the deacon's words at Mass are a command: "Give one another peace." In English, the translation is more exhortatory: "Let us offer each other the sign of peace." That is the formula that the early draft proposed in Latin when a lay minister presided, clearly including the minister among those giving the exchange of peace. In the end, the alternate formula for a lay minister was removed, but in English, even at Mass, the exhortatory translation of the command remains.

[60] Schema 401 (37), p. 11; Schema 403 (18), p. 14; and Schema 405 (18), p. 14.

[61] Schema 401 (38), p. 11; Schema 403 (19), p. 15; and Schema 405 (19), p. 15.

The minister genuflects, takes a host, and holds it over the vessel while making the same invitation the priest uses at Mass (OM 132), "Behold the Lamb of God . . ." The communicants respond as at Mass, "Lord, I am not worthy . . ." (HC 32). If the minister will also be receiving communion, the minister joins in the reply, as the priest always does at Mass. If not, the minister remains silent. Both at Mass and in this ritual the rubrics contain two superfluous details: the minister faces the people, and the communicants make their response only once. The minister naturally faces the people at a freestanding altar. The reply was made three times in the preconciliar rubrics, but the repetition has been removed, so this reminder is no longer necessary.

In the missal, the priest may hold the host over the paten or over the chalice (OM 132). The minister has only one option at HC 32 because there is no chalice on the altar. At Mass many priests raise the paten or chalice with the other hand, but the rubric never asks them to do so. In the preconciliar Mass, holding the host above the paten while facing the people, the priest had to use both hands, but with a freestanding altar he may hold the host over the vessel that rests upon the altar. The minister at HC 32 may do the same.

This is the second genuflection: one has occurred upon placing the vessel on the altar, and the other occurs before the invitation, "Behold the Lamb of God." At Mass, the priest genuflects twice during the consecration and a third time just before communion. In all instances, he is showing reverence toward the real presence of the Body and Blood of Christ. At Mass, his reverence also functions as part of his own preparation to receive communion. At this ritual, the minister genuflects in reverence before distributing communion to others, whether or not the minister receives.

In the Roman Ritual predating these changes, the priest was to hold the host with his thumb and forefinger. This detail has been removed, though it is the natural way for a minister to hold the host. Then, in the former practice, the priest said both parts of the dialogue: "Behold the Lamb of God," and "Lord, I am not worthy." The communicants had no obligatory speaking parts during the celebration. In Latin, the adjective "worthy" was gender specific. The priest was required to use the masculine form even if he recited the words on behalf of a woman receiving communion.[62]

The 1969 draft assigned the response to all, omitting all rubrical instructions (3). The other drafts supplied the words for the dialogue, but omitted any reference to a genuflection.[63]

If the minister will receive communion, he or she prepares with a short prayer (HC 33). As a priest does at Mass (OM 133), the minister recites quietly the words, "May the Body of Christ keep me safe for eternal life." The instruction occurred in all of the drafts. In most of them, the minister was instructed to turn toward the altar, presuming it was fixed against the wall.[64] In the final version, the directional instruction was removed, probably because it was unnecessary.

The minister approaches those to receive communion, slightly raises a host over the vessel before each in turn, shows it, and declares, "The Body of Christ." These imitate the rubrics assigned to a priest distributing communion at Mass (GIRM 161). The communicant replies "Amen" and receives (HC 34). Similar rubrics appeared in all the drafts,[65] though with little detail in the one from 1969 (3). In the Roman Ritual, the communicant made no reply, and the priest recited a longer formula in Latin with each communion: "May the Body of our Lord Jesus Christ keep your soul safe for eternal life. Amen."

[62] *Rituale Romanum*, Titulus V, Caput II:3, p. 155.

[63] Schema 401 (39–40), pp. 11–12; Schema 403 (20), p. 15; and Schema 405 (20), p. 15.

[64] Schema 401 (41), p. 12; Schema 403 (21), p. 15; and Schema 405 (21), p. 15.

[65] Schema 401 (42), p. 12; Schema 403 (22), p. 15; and Schema 405 (22), p. 15.

He also made the sign of the cross with the host in his hand; that gesture has been removed even from the Mass.

A song may be sung during the distribution of communion (HC 35). The Roman Ritual indicated no music, but at the conclusion of distributing communion, the priest was to recite the hymn *O sacrum convivium*, now found among antiphons at HC 200 and in the communion of the sick in HC 65. An early draft suggested singing or reading a communion antiphon from the missal or *O sacrum convivium* during the distribution of communion outside Mass.[66] The other drafts permitted a song but offered no recommendations.[67] In all these cases, the song "may" be sung, making some other song or even silence a viable option. During Mass, a communion antiphon or song is obligatory (GIRM 87), but not outside Mass.

After distributing communion, if all the hosts have been consumed, the minister collects any fragments that may remain into the ciborium, presumably to be cleansed after the service. The minister may then wash his or her hands. However, if hosts remain, then the minister places them in the ciborium, returns it to the tabernacle, and genuflects (HC 36). Presumably, the minister then closes the door. According to the missal, at the end of the Mass of the Lord's Supper on Holy Thursday, the ministers kneel in adoration at the place of repose, the priest incenses the Sacrament, and then the deacon or priest places the ciborium in the tabernacle and closes the door (Roman Missal, Holy Thursday 39). Similarly, outside Mass, a genuflection would be appropriate before the door is closed.

At Mass, a priest may wash his "fingers" after communion if any fragments adhere to them (GIRM 278). In an early draft, citing the same passage in the GIRM, the minister used a cloth to wipe his or her "fingers" and the paten over a ciborium or

[66] Schema 401 (43), p. 12.

[67] Schema 403 (23), p. 15; and Schema 405 (23), p. 15.

other vessel.[68] The other drafts and HC 36 removed the reference to the cloth but allowed the minister to purify his or her "hands."[69] Perhaps the word changed because there is no breaking of bread outside Mass. As at Mass, the rubrics anticipate that this is not a regular concern.

The Roman Ritual required the priest diligently to take notice that if any fragment adhered to his fingers, he would place it in the ciborium and then place the fingers that touched the sacrament into a vessel of water. Afterward, he poured the water into the sacrarium or into fire.[70]

The same late drafts had the minister put any fragments found on the paten into the ciborium.[71] However, they did not call for the purification of that vessel or its placement back into the tabernacle if it contained not just fragments, but hosts.

The minister puts "fragments" into the ciborium but "hosts" into the tabernacle. At Mass, "fragments" are collected before the vessel is purified (GIRM 163, 183, 278). In the missal, the same Latin word that HC 36 translates as "hosts" refers to the "small piece" of the broken host that the priest puts into the chalice (GIRM 155, OM 129) or part of a broken host that concelebrants consume at their communion (GIRM 249). It is also the term used when describing care for a fallen host or "particle" of one (GIRM 280). In the missal, a "particle" is something larger than a "fragment," but in HC 21 "particle" refers to a host. Here, the plural of the same Latin word is translated "hosts" for clarity.

All may then observe silence, or a psalm or canticle of praise may be sung (HC 37). The rubric does not specify who sings, so it could be all, a few, or a solo cantor. At Mass a similar rubric is at GIRM 164 and OM 138, though GIRM 88 permits a song sung by the entire congregation.

[68] Schema 401 (44), p. 12.

[69] Schema 403 (24), p. 15; and Schema 405 (24), p. 15.

[70] *Rituale Romanum*, Titulus V, Caput II:8, p. 157.

[71] Schema 403 (24), p. 15; and Schema 405 (24), p. 15.

The Roman Ritual did not offer the option of silence. As noted above, the priest recited *O sacrum convivium* after communion and before the purification. He then led a dialogue with the minister, *Panem de cælo*, citing Wisdom 16:20: "You have given them bread from heaven"—to which the minister responded, "Having all sweetness within it." The priest and the minister each added an alleluia at the end of their words during Easter Time. The dialogue continued in Latin with the opening verse from Psalm 102: "O Lord, hear my prayer." "And let my cry come to you." The priest greeted the minister in the customary way, "The Lord be with you." The minister responded, "And with your spirit." The priest said the prayer.[72]

The drafts permitted silence or song to replace the Roman Ritual's *O sacrum convivium* after communion.[73] The minister preserved the *Panem de cælo* dialogue, but with one alternative word in the early draft: "You have given them bread from heaven," or "You have given us bread from heaven," which applied the words of the book of Wisdom to the gathered assembly.

The same draft approved alternative versicles in dialogue,[74] the examples coming from its rite of Benediction: "Your children, O Lord, [are] like shoots of the olive around your table," applying the words of Psalm 128:3 to the community gathered at the Lord's table. Or, "Let us adore Christ the King, who gives richness of spirit to those eating him," taken from the preconciliar invitatory antiphon at Matins on Corpus Christi. For Easter Time, the early draft recommended, "Christ, our Passover, has been sacrificed, alleluia. Therefore, let us feast on the Lord, alleluia," based on 1 Corinthians 5:7-8.[75]

[72] *Rituale Romanum*, Titulus V, Caput II:6–7, p. 156.

[73] Schema 401 (45), p. 12; Schema 403 (25), p. 15; and Schema 405 (25), p. 15.

[74] Schema 401 (46, 47), p. 12.

[75] Schema 401 (91), p. 25.

The other drafts kept only the traditional *Panem de cælo*, with the change from "given them" to "given us."[76] HC 37 removed this dialogue, leaving behind only the options for silence or a hymn.

The minister says a concluding prayer (HC 38). The first recommended is the collect from the Mass of the Most Holy Body and Blood of Christ, a prayer that the priest recited after distributing communion to the people in the Roman Ritual.[77] The words focus on the real presence of Christ, rather than the enduring fruits of communion from the sacrifice, as is common in prayers after communion at Mass. This prayer reappears after communion in a brief celebration of communion outside Mass (50) and at the end of Benediction (98). During Easter Time, the Roman Ritual changed that prayer to the one that now serves as the prayer after communion at the Easter Vigil. It may still be used as an alternative, though it is not limited to Easter Time (211).

The 1969 draft permitted either a song or a prayer of thanksgiving after communion (3). The subsequent drafts called for both. They also allowed silence after the minister's invitation, "Let us pray," as in OM 139 and GIRM 135.[78] However, HC 38 removed the option, probably because the optional silence before "Let us pray" seemed sufficient.

An early draft did not supply a specific prayer after communion, but invited the minister to use the one from the same day in the missal, "having made any necessary change if the same prayer makes any mention of the eucharistic celebration enacted immediately before or of the solemnity or the feast in a way that would not perhaps be fitting for the rite."[79] The other drafts provided the traditional collect of Corpus Christi,

[76] Schema 403 (26), p. 16; and Schema 405 (26), p. 16.

[77] *Rituale Romanum*, Titulus V, Caput II:7, p. 156.

[78] Schema 401 (48), p. 13; Schema 403 (26), p. 16; and Schema 405 (26), p. 16.

[79] Schema 401 (48), p. 13.

while permitting ten more options.[80] All of those remain in HC and in the same order:

- The collect for the votive Mass of the Most Holy Eucharist (HC 210)
- The prayer after communion from the Easter Vigil (HC 211), which the Roman Ritual offered as the only alternative and reserved for Easter Time
- The prayer after communion for the votive Mass of the Most Holy Eucharist (HC 212)
- The prayer after communion for Tuesday and Friday of the first three weeks of Advent, and for the Second Sunday of Advent (HC 213)
- The prayer after communion for the Second Sunday of Lent (HC 214)
- The prayer after communion for the First Week in Ordinary Time (HC 215), which Bugnini said was the only one of the list not found in the missal of 1970, though it is there[81]
- The prayer after communion for the Fifth Sunday in Ordinary Time (HC 216)
- The prayer after communion for the Twenty-Second Sunday in Ordinary Time (HC 217)
- The prayer after communion for the Thirty-Second Sunday in Ordinary Time (HC 218)
- And the prayer after communion from the Common of Martyrs during Easter Time, the second of the choices for several martyrs (HC 219)

[80] Schema 403, pp. 33–34; and Schema 405, pp. 33–34.

[81] Bugnini, p. 663, fn. 79.

Although the usage of these no longer needs to correspond to the liturgical times of year, they may. After the prayer, the people answer, "Amen."

The Concluding Rites

Directions for the concluding rites depend on the minister. A priest or deacon gives a blessing to the people, whereas a lay minister invokes God's blessing upon all including the minister (HC 39–40).

A priest or deacon introduces the familiar dialogue, "The Lord be with you," and then offers the blessing formula from the end of Mass (OM 141). He may insert a solemn blessing or prayer over the people from the Roman Missal (HC 39). The rubric calls for him to face the people and extend his hands, instructions probably copied without forethought from the Order of Mass. Assigning the direction to face is unnecessary because the priest or deacon has probably returned to his chair, which, at least at Mass, is to face the people (GIRM 310). Indeed, the direction is missing from the instructions for the lay minister's concluding rites, presuming that this minister is already facing the people.

In that case, the lay minister signs himself or herself while saying the words invoking God's blessing and protection. Two options are given. To either of them, all answer, "Amen" (HC 40).

In the Roman Ritual the priest began the blessing by raising his eyes while extending, lifting, and joining his hands. Then he bowed his head to the cross, turned to the people, and gave the traditional trinitarian formula of the blessing. This blessing was omitted if communion of the faithful took place during Mass, which concluded with its own blessing.[82] The post-

[82] *Rituale Romanum*, Titulus V, Caput II:9, p. 157.

conciliar reform removed the raising of eyes, the circular gesture of the hands, and the bow to the cross.

The 1969 draft made no reference to a blessing, but the other drafts concur that a priest or a deacon used the formula from Mass. He greeted the people and recited the blessing, which might be augmented with a solemn form. The two formulas offered to lay ministers in the final version came unchanged from the later drafts.[83] An early draft offered a different option, "Let us bless the Lord," to which all those present answered, "Thanks be to God." The first of the remaining formulas also concludes Morning and Evening Prayer in the Ordinary of the Liturgy of the Hours when a layperson presides.

As in the rubrics for Mass, there is no indication that the faithful sign themselves with the cross when either a cleric or a lay minister says the words of blessing. Most people usually do anyway. It is hard to discern if this simply carries over the same omission from the preconciliar rubrics, which gave very few instructions for the people, or if they intend for the people simply to receive the blessing without signing themselves. Before proclaiming the gospel, when a deacon asks the priest for a blessing, the deacon is to sign himself as he hears the names of the Trinity, and to answer "Amen" (OM 14). Even so, it is hard to discern if omitting the people's sign of the cross is an oversight or deliberate.

At the end, the minister dismisses the people with the words, "Go in peace." The people reply, "Thanks be to God" (HC 41). Although many English-speaking Catholics are accustomed to hearing that dismissal at the end of Mass (OM 144), in Latin the words are different: The people are commanded simply to "go," but the English translation softens this single syllable by adding "in peace." For communion outside Mass, the Latin adds the words "in peace" to enrich the

[83] Schema 401 (49–51), p. 16; Schema 403 (27), p. 16; and Schema 405 (27), p. 16.

bare command that remains after omitting the rest of the formula, "*missa est*." This is not Mass, so the people must be sent forth with other words.

Only the later drafts included the dismissal formula. The words are unchanged, but at first they were restricted to a priest or deacon.[84] HC 41 allows any minister to say, "Go in peace."

The minister makes a sign of reverence and leaves (HC 41). The nature of the reverence is not specified. It probably means a bow to the altar. If the tabernacle is in the sanctuary, then the reverences from GIRM 274 would logically apply: A genuflection to the tabernacle would conclude the service. As at Mass, the rubrics instruct ministers to leave, but are silent about the people. In practice they do leave at the minister's command. All the drafts instructed the minister to make a reverence before leaving.[85]

This order of service provides a cogent celebration for the people. It gives due respect to the proclamation of Sacred Scripture before the distribution of communion. It borrows many rubrics and words from the celebration of the Mass, with which the people are familiar, from which the celebration derives, and toward which it is ultimately directed.

The Order of Distributing Holy Communion outside Mass: The Rite with a Brief Celebration of the Word of God

The preceding ritual envisions a number of communicants and presents itself as an ordinary way to distribute communion outside Mass. However, when there are only one or two communicants who are healthy, the celebration changes. This ceremony fills the need (HC 42). It more closely resembles the

[84] Schema 403 (28), p. 17; and Schema 405 (28), p. 17.

[85] Schema 401 (51), p. 13; Schema 403 (28), p. 17; and Schema 405 (28), p. 17.

distribution of communion before or after Mass prior to the liturgical reforms. The rubrics presume it takes place in church at the altar.

The drafts envisioned something simple. The 1969 draft began with John 6:55-57 or another short passage. Then it proceeded to the Lord's Prayer and the distribution of communion (3).

The next draft envisioned omitting "the reading and those things connected to it," probably the psalm and the homily. It also omitted the universal prayer, the sign of peace, and a period of silence. It kept the penitential act, the Lord's Prayer, and the formula for showing and administering communion, as well as the final prayer with its verse, the blessing and dismissal.[86] The subsequent drafts opened with the same notice now appearing as HC 42, explaining its purpose.[87]

The Introductory Rites

The ceremony begins in the same way as the fuller celebration (HC 43). The arrangements noted in numbers 19 and 20 are to have been completed. Without entrance music, the minister greets the communicants as described in 27 or 189. The minister introduces the penitential act as in 28, 190, and 191. The drafts gave similar instructions.[88]

The fuller celebration gave a nod to the Order of Mass with its opening rubric, "When the faithful are gathered," but this liturgy has only one or two communicants. No congregation is envisioned, so no echo of the opening rubric for Mass is provided. No presider's chair is indicated.

The drafts all included a penitential act, but the one from 1969 placed it after the Lord's Prayer as in its fuller celebration,

[86] Schema 401 (52), p. 13.

[87] Schema 403 (29), p. 17; and Schema 405 (29), p. 17.

[88] Schema 401 (52), p. 13; Schema 403 (30), p. 17; and Schema 405 (30), p. 17.

in imitation of the practice that had been common before the reforms. An early draft specified that the penitential act was never to be omitted. The other drafts included it without further comment.[89]

The Shorter Reading of the Word of God

The minister or another person then reads one or a few verses from the Bible making mention of the bread of life (HC 44). The specific suggestion from 1969 (John 6:55-57) disappeared from the other drafts. The last ones advised a reading referring to the Bread of Life,[90] which would have included the earlier recommendation. The final version included several suggestions, not all of which directly mention the Bread of Life:

- John 6:54-55, where Jesus promises eternal life to those who eat his flesh and drink his blood
- John 6:54-58, a longer passage from the same discourse, where Jesus calls himself the bread that came down from heaven
- John 14:6, where Jesus proclaims himself the way, the truth, and the life
- John 14:23, where Jesus states that the one who loves him will keep his word
- John 15:4, where Jesus promises to remain with those who remain in him
- 1 Corinthians 11:26, where Paul says that to eat the bread and drink the cup as at the Supper is to announce the death of the Lord

[89] Schema 401 (52), p. 13; Schema 403 (30), p. 17; and Schema 405 (30), p. 17.

[90] Schema 403 (31), p. 17; and Schema 405 (31), p. 17.

Any of the passages listed in the fourth chapter may also be used (HC 113-188). These come from the missal's votive Masses of the Most Holy Eucharist or of the Most Precious Blood of Our Lord Jesus Christ, and of the Most Sacred Heart of Jesus, as noted above.

Holy Communion

The minister takes the vessel with the consecrated hosts, places it on the altar, and genuflects. The minister then introduces the Lord's Prayer (HC 45), using the formula from Mass (OM 124). All recite the prayer together.

The drafts all included the Lord's Prayer. The 1969 draft allowed the entire ceremony to begin here if circumstances suggested (5). The early draft alone stated that the Lord's Prayer was never to be omitted in the short form.[91] The minister's introduction appeared in the later drafts and remains unchanged in HC 45. Unlike at Mass, the rubric clearly states that the introduction may be given in similar words.

The sign of peace is omitted; only two or three people are present. An early draft explicitly called for the omission of the sign, whereas the later drafts included it.[92] HC 45 and 46 omit any reference to it, so it is understood to be excluded.

The minister genuflects a second time, raises a host above the vessel, and introduces the dialogue before communion (HC 46), as in the fuller form (32). The dialogue can be found in the later drafts.[93] Even this rubric copies from OM 132 the instruction that the minister faces the communicant for the dialogue, which should be obvious. If the minister is going to

[91] Schema 401 (52), p. 13; Schema 403 (31), p. 17; and Schema 405 (31), p. 17.

[92] Schema 401 (52), p. 13; Schema 403 (32), p. 17; and Schema 405 (32), p. 17.

[93] Schema 403 (33), p. 18; and Schema 405 (33), p. 18.

receive communion, he or she joins in the response that begins, "Lord, I am not worthy."

If the minister is to receive communion, he or she quietly recites the private preparation that the priest says at Mass (HC 47), as in the fuller form (33), and then consumes the host. The late drafts indicated that the minister consumed communion facing the altar,[94] but this was removed from the final version, which presumes a freestanding altar at which the minister stands and from which the people are visible.

The minister goes to the communicants and gives communion (HC 48) with the usual formula as in the fuller form (34). The drafts also always included the dialogue that accompanies communion: "The Body of Christ." "Amen."[95] No communion hymn is indicated, probably because this service may only involve two people, one administering and one receiving communion.

The minister handles any remaining fragments and particles (HC 49) as in the fuller form (36). The drafts similarly repeated the instructions from the equivalent place.[96]

Silence or song may follow as in the fuller form (HC 37). The drafts did not envision song here, though they did provide the text for the *Panem de cælo* dialogue.[97] As in the fuller form, it has been removed.

The minister offers a concluding prayer (HC 50), taken from the collect for the solemnity of the Most Holy Body and Blood of Christ as in the fuller form (38). (It reappears at 98 as the first recommended after the blessing in worship of the Eucharist outside Mass.) All of the same alternatives to this prayer are available in this form as well (210–222). The drafts had included no spoken prayer. In the late drafts, the minister said,

[94] Schema 403 (34), p. 18; and Schema 405 (34), p. 18.

[95] Schema 401 (52), p. 13; Schema 403 (35) p. 18; and Schema 405 (35), p. 18.

[96] Schema 403 (36), p. 18; and Schema 405 (36), p. 18.

[97] Schema 403 (37), p. 18; and Schema 405 (37), p. 18.

"Let us pray," but then the rubric explained that "if appropriate, all pray in silence for a period of time."[98] A spoken prayer brings closure to the act of communion.

The Concluding Rites

The service concludes with a blessing and dismissal (HC 51–53). These repeat those in the fuller form (HC 39–41), except for the omission of a solemn blessing or prayer over the people when a priest or deacon presides. The drafts had permitted such an expanded blessing in the short form,[99] but the final version removed it. The simpler form of blessing prevails.

As in the fuller form, the drafts restricted the dismissal formula to a priest or deacon.[100] The final version permits any minister to dismiss the people before making a sign of reverence and leaving. As in the missal, an appropriate sign of reverence would be a bow to the altar or a genuflection to the tabernacle if it is located in the sanctuary (GIRM 274).

In all, this would be a rare circumstance when a minister would meet a single or a very few faithful Catholics in church for a communion service. However, the drafts all imagined the possibility, and HC includes it.

An early draft proposed another form for distributing communion: within a celebration of the Liturgy of the Hours. During Lauds and Vespers, it permitted communion after the Lord's Prayer. The gospel canticle, which usually precedes the Lord's Prayer, could have been sung after communion instead, or, leaving it in place, communion could have been followed by a period of silence. In the office of readings, the draft permitted the distribution of communion after the second reading and its response, before the final prayer. A song from the

98 Schema 403 (37), p. 18; and Schema 405 (37), p. 18.

99 Schema 403 (38), p. 19; and Schema 405 (38), p. 19.

100 Schema 403 (39), p. 19; and Schema 405 (39), p. 19.

appendix of the Liturgy of the Hours could then have been sung. At daytime prayer, communion would follow the short reading and its verse. In the office of readings and in daytime prayer, the penitential act and the Lord's Prayer could have been added.[101] Subsequent drafts removed this entire section. The distribution of communion does not take place during the Liturgy of the Hours.

[101] Schema 401 (53–55), p. 14.

Administration of Communion and Viaticum to the Sick by an Extraordinary Minister

Many Catholics falsely assume that "last rites" may only be administered by a priest and are to be given as close to death as possible. But the most important "last rite," Viaticum, may be administered by a priest, a deacon, an instituted acolyte, or a deputed lay minister of Holy Communion, a category with which many parishes teem.

Chapter II of HC explains how lay ministers bring communion to the sick under normal circumstances and when the sick person is dying. A priest or a deacon uses a different book, *Pastoral Care of the Sick: Rites of Anointing and Viaticum* (HC 54).

An acolyte is a layperson, male or female, whom the bishop, an ordinary, or his delegate has instituted into this stable ministry. Extraordinary ministers of Holy Communion are more common in parishes and frequently assist in the distribution of communion at Mass. They are to be deputed for this ministry at the direction of the bishop and appointed in a prayer service from the *Book of Blessings*.[1]

In permitting lay ministers to offer Viaticum, the Church makes the sacrament as available as possible to those who are near death. In the fourth century the Council of Nicaea tolerated giving Viaticum even to an unforgiven penitent, according

[1] Paul Turner, *Present for God's Call: An Overview of the Rites of Institution and Ordination* (Chicago: Liturgy Training Publications, 2022), pp. 18–32.

to what it considered an old canonical law still in force.[2] In the sixth century the dying St. Benedict asked his disciples to carry him to the oratory to be strengthened with the Body and Blood of Christ—perhaps administered by his own hand.[3] The Council of Toledo in 675 recommended the administration of Viaticum by dipping the consecrated bread into the consecrated wine so that the faithful could more easily receive.[4] The Roman Orders of the seventh and eighth centuries gave more details on the rites of Viaticum, including the recitation of part of the passion in conjunction with the administration of communion.[5] A pastoral note in the French translation of the postconciliar rite suggests that one of the dying person's communions, not necessarily the last, may take on this special meaning at a Mass with appropriate readings, prayers, and administration of both the Body and Blood of Christ.[6] By separating Viaticum from the absolute moments before death, the minister is more likely to offer this sacrament, which may be repeated if dying is prolonged.

A priest may celebrate Mass in the presence of the sick and offer anointing and communion within the single ceremony. An early draft of HC joined in promoting this.[7] Historically, a priest ideally offered communion to the sick during Mass. Sometimes the sick were brought to church, or the priest celebrated Mass in their home. The most convenient method has always been to bring communion to the sick outside Mass.[8]

Communion may be administered to the sick under the form of wine alone if they are not able to chew. The early drafts cited

[2] Martimort II, p. 236, and Rouillard, p. 288.

[3] Rouillard, p. 288.

[4] Rouillard, pp. 288–89.

[5] Rouillard, p. 289.

[6] Rouillard, p. 292, citing *Sacraments pour les Malades: Pastorale et célébrations* (Chalet—Tardy, 1977), no. 145, p. 92.

[7] Schema 401 (65 and 67), p. 16.

[8] Martimort II, p. 237.

EM 41 as the source of this permission.[9] The vessel needs to be sealed so as to prevent spillage. A proper vessel would be a flask sealed with a screw top, for example. In Mass kits, retailers sell vessels for transporting water and wine; one of these could be used. In practice, before Mass, the chosen vessel may be filled with a small amount of wine and set with the gifts to be brought to the altar. The priest may remove the lid and consecrate the wine in the vessel. At communion time, he may secure the lid again. After communion, he may either place the vessel in the hands of a communion minister, or, if he himself is going to administer communion after Mass, place it temporarily in the tabernacle. Consecrated wine may not otherwise be stored in the tabernacle.[10]

After administering communion, if any of the Precious Blood remains, the minister consumes it before cleansing the vessel (HC 55). As when administering communion at church outside Mass (22), the Latin word for this final action is *ablutiones*, which the English version translates as "purifications," a word generally reserved for the cleansing of vessels at Mass, though it will reappear at HC 62 in both Latin and English.

Canon law forbids an individual from keeping the Eucharist on one's person or carrying it around without pastoral necessity (canon 935). A minister going to visit the sick is to go directly from the tabernacle to the person.

The Ordinary Rite of Communion of the Sick

An early draft requested two versions of communion to the sick, one dealing with communion of a single sick person, and the other with the communion of many who are sick in a

[9] Schema 401 (65), p. 16.

[10] *Norms for the Distribution and Reception of Holy Communion under Both Kinds in the Dioceses of the United States* (Washington, DC: United States Conference of Catholic Bishops, 2002), par. 54.

hospital.[11] The later drafts did not include the distinction. The final version of HC restored the idea under the titles of "ordinary" and "short" rites.

The Introductory Rites

The minister wears whatever vesture is appropriate, as indicated in the introduction (HC 20). Approaching the sick person, the minister offers a friendly greeting (56). This resembles the instruction for a priest to greet a penitent (Order of Penance 41), intended to decrease tension in a potentially emotional situation.

This opening borrows heavily from the Ordinary Rite of Communion of the Sick among the rites for their anointing and pastoral care by a priest or a deacon (PCS 81, or 49 in the Latin edition). He also is to vest appropriately and to greet the sick with friendly words. The recommended greeting, "Peace to this house and all here," is the first option for a priest or deacon to say. It comes from Jesus's sending of the seventy-two disciples, who were to use these words first upon entering a house (Luke 10:5). The lay minister may use other words of greeting from Scripture, as indicated when distributing communion at church outside Mass (HC 27). At Viaticum, though, the lay minister may use the greeting from Luke (68).

In the Roman Ritual, the same greeting appeared, but in dialogue form. The priest said in Latin, "Peace be to this house," and a server responded in Latin, "And to all who dwell here."[12] The same division appeared in an early draft of HC,[13] but the final version assigns the entire verse to the minister, which is a more practical idea.

[11] Schema 401 (heading to 56), p. 14.

[12] *Rituale Romanum*, Titulus V, Caput IV:14, p. 163.

[13] Schema 401 (62), p. 15.

The minister sets the Sacrament on a table where all may adore it (HC 56). This too comes from the ritual for a priest (PCS 81, or 49 in the Latin edition). However, the priest may then sprinkle the sick person and the room with blessed water (PCS 82, or 50 in the Latin edition).

The Roman Ritual had likewise included a brief period of adoration. A corporal was first placed on the table. The priest genuflected, and all present knelt down. The priest sprinkled the sick person and the room with blessed water while leading in Latin the antiphon "Sprinkle me with hyssop, O Lord, and I shall be cleansed; you will wash me and I shall be whiter than snow." He then offered the first verse of Psalm 51, the "Glory Be" to the Trinity, the repetition of the antiphon, and a dialogue with the minister: "Our help is in the name of the Lord." "Who made heaven and earth." "O Lord, hear my prayer." "And let my cry come to you." "The Lord be with you." "And with your spirit."[14]

The first draft kept the genuflection, but the others removed it. It retained the sprinkling with its antiphons, verses, and dialogue if the minister were a priest or deacon.[15] Today a priest or deacon uses a shorter formula for the sprinkling, but local rituals may propose other options for him (PCS 82, or 50 in the Latin edition). The final version of HC has removed the sprinkling and any accompanying words when a lay minister presides, possibly because at Sunday Mass, according to the second appendix of the Roman Missal, a priest is the one who may sprinkle blessed water.

The minister introduces the penitential act (HC 57), as a priest does at Mass (OM 6) or in communion to the sick (PCS 83, or 52 in the Latin edition). The alternative introductions for distributing communion at church outside Mass apply here as well (HC 28).

[14] *Rituale Romanum*, Titulus V, Caput IV:15, pp. 163–164.

[15] Schema 401 (63), p. 16.

The Roman Ritual encouraged the priest to hear the confession of the sick person,[16] which an early draft also suggested,[17] and which is still an option when a priest brings communion to the sick (PCS 82, or 51 in the Latin edition). A lay minister leads a penitential act.

The Shorter Reading of the Word of God

Even for the sick, communion is not administered without at least a short reading from the Bible (HC 58). A member of the family or friend in attendance may read a passage, or the minister may do so. Any passage is acceptable, but a selection of options appears in the administration of Viaticum (71). These are identical to the ones from the brief rite of administering communion to one or two persons at church (44), but with three additional options:

- John 14:27, where Jesus bestows peace on his disciples at the Last Supper
- John 15:5, where Jesus declares on the same occasion that he is the vine, they the branches
- 1 John 4:16, about coming to know the love of God for the individual

These are suggestions. The minister may select a different passage.

The Roman Ritual included no Scripture reading. An early draft implied it could be omitted in a shorter form of the rite.[18] Now some reading is expected.

[16] *Rituale Romanum*, Titulus V, Caput IV:16, p. 164.
[17] Schema 401 (64), p. 16.
[18] Schema 401 (56), p. 14.

Holy Communion

The minister introduces the Lord's Prayer. The formula comes from the priest's ritual (PCS 87, or 54 in the Latin edition), but the minister may choose other words. All recite the Lord's Prayer (HC 59), as in administering Holy Communion outside Mass (HC 30).

The Roman Ritual had not included the Lord's Prayer before the priest administered communion to the sick. Now it is considered part of the communion rite.

The minister shows the Sacrament to the sick person and introduces the dialogue that begins with "Behold the Lamb of God" and "Lord, I am not worthy" (HC 60) as in administering communion outside Mass (32). The sign of peace that precedes the administration of communion at church is omitted (31).

In the Roman Ritual, the priest genuflected before showing the host to the sick person. He led the same dialogue, though the custom at the time was to repeat the response "Lord, I am not worthy" three times. A sick person was allowed to say it only once, and in a low voice.[19]

The minister goes to the sick person, again shows the host, and says, "The Body of Christ." If communion is under the form of wine, the minister says, "The Blood of Christ," and the sick person responds, "Amen" before receiving communion. Others may receive communion in the usual way (HC 61).

The minister purifies the vessel, and all may observe silence (HC 62). In this case and in administering Viaticum (77), both in Latin and in English, the word is "purification," even when a layperson performs the action. This differs from the Latin word in HC 55. In practice, the minister puts water into the vessel and drinks it.

The minister leads the concluding prayer (HC 62), which is copied from the administration of communion to the sick by a priest (PCS 90C, or 57 in the Latin edition). It comes from the

[19] *Rituale Romanum*, Titulus V, Caput IV:18.

same ceremony in the Roman Ritual, with a slight change in word order. In the Roman Ritual, the prayer differentiated between a male or female person receiving communion, and even offered plural versions. Although HC 62 in Latin just refers to "our brother," the English translation distinguishes whether the individual receiving communion is a "brother" or a "sister." The Roman Ritual also used a different ending; instead of "Through Christ our Lord," it had "who lives and reigns with you in the unity of the Holy Spirit, God for ever and ever."[20] The relative pronoun "who" may be used because of the proximity of the name of Christ near the end of the prayer, but the longer ending is now generally reserved for a collect or the oration that concludes Morning and Evening Prayer. The words also change to identify properly the administration of the Body or Blood of Christ. The minister may replace this entire prayer with a choice from the same alternatives available when administering communion outside Mass (HC 38, 50).

The Concluding Rites

The minister invokes God's blessing and signs himself or herself with the cross, while offering one of two formulas (HC 63), as in the distribution of communion outside Mass (40). All answer "Amen."

The Roman Ritual had the priest end the ceremony a different way. If some hosts remained, he put on the humeral veil, genuflected, arose, covered the pyx with the humeral veil, and made the sign of the cross over the sick person, saying nothing. Then he returned to church reciting psalms and hymns. At the church, he led the *Panem de cælo* dialogue, greeted the assisting minister, recited the prayer that served as the collect on Corpus Christi, announced the indulgences available, made the sign

[20] *Rituale Romanum*, Titulus V, Caput IV:22, p. 166.

of the cross over the people with the pyx in silence, and placed the Sacrament back into the tabernacle. Alternatively, in the presence of the sick person he could have consumed the hosts that remained and blessed the person with his hand, using the traditional formula.[21] In the revised rite for priests, all that remains is for him to give a blessing with a formula like those at Mass, or, in silence, to make the sign of the cross over the people with the pyx containing the remaining hosts (PCS 91, or 58 in the Latin edition).

The Short Rite of Communion of the Sick

In an institution such as a hospital, where numerous sick people occupy different rooms of the same building, a minister of Holy Communion may use this shorter form of the rite (HC 64). It places the visits to all the rooms into a single liturgy, but it may seem perfunctory for the sick.

The Roman Ritual had made provision for this as well. The priest began in one room, using the plural form of the prayers. In each room, he led the penitential prayers and distributed communion with the formulas. In the last room, he led the final sections of the rite, using the plural form.[22]

An early draft of this ritual suggested the use of radio transmission. If the hospital had the necessary equipment, the minister could begin the ceremony in one room while transmitting it to others, proceed to those individual rooms for distribution, and conclude with transmission to them all. This draft also permitted other clergy, religious sisters, and laymen and laywomen to assist the priest or deacon in distributing communion to the rooms, thus shortening the time for the entire ceremony.[23] The same draft then offered this option: "The

[21] *Rituale Romanum*, Titulus V, Caput IV:23–27, pp. 166–167.

[22] *Rituale Romanum*, Titulus V, Caput IV:28, pp. 167–168.

[23] Schema 401 (58) p. 15.

preparation of the sick for receiving communion may at times take place through a radio broadcast of the Mass. At the time when communion takes place at Mass, it may be distributed to the sick, using many ministers as indicated above."[24]

This was never approved. However, during the height of the COVID-19 pandemic, some parishes livestreamed a Mass to faithful scattered outdoors or indoors, who could not gather in large groups, and ministers distributed communion during the rite. This received some criticism for not fully engaging the active participation of the people.[25]

An early draft envisioned the ordinary would appoint religious sisters or appropriate laymen or women to prepare the sick for communion in different parts of the hospital. "Rarely should everything be reduced to the single formula of offering the host, omitting the rest."[26]

In HC 65, the minister begins the ceremony in a church, chapel, or the first room, and recites the antiphon "O sacred banquet" (*O sacrum convivium*). The words, attributed to St. Thomas Aquinas, are the traditional Magnificat antiphon from second Vespers of Corpus Christi, now retained in the same place for Evening Prayer in the Liturgy of the Hours for the solemnity of the Most Holy Body and Blood of Christ.

Another antiphon may replace this one. The drafts listed *O sacrum convivium* as the first of four alternatives in their third chapter.[27] All of these now appear in the same order in the fourth chapter (HC 200–203), among other various texts to be used.

[24] Schema 401 (59), p. 15.

[25] Paul Turner, "What's Happened to the Liturgy: Liturgical Adaptations Prompted by COVID," Southwest Liturgical Conference, February 2, 2021, p. 8, https://paulturner.org/wp-content/uploads/2021/03/SWLC-COVID.pdf.

[26] Schema 401 (60–61), p. 15.

[27] Schema 403, p. 31; and Schema 405, p. 31.

The second option (HC 201), *O quam suavis est*, is the traditional Magnificat antiphon from first Vespers of Corpus Christi, preserved in the same place in the Liturgy of the Hours for the solemnity of the Most Holy Body and Blood of Christ. It alludes to several biblical passages: Exodus 16:4, where the Lord promised the Israelites a rainfall of manna, a bread from heaven; Psalms 78:24 and 105:40, which also call manna a bread from heaven; Wisdom 16:20-21, which tells of God sharing the sweet heavenly bread of the angels with his children; and Luke 1:53, part of Mary's Magnificat, which praises God who, having filled the hungry with good things, sends the rich away empty.

The third option (HC 202) is *Ave verum Corpus*, a hymn from the Middle Ages addressing the true Body of Christ, present in the form of the consecrated bread. It was listed among the chants suitable for Benediction in the *Liber Usualis*, a collection of music for the divine office and other services.[28]

The last option (HC 203), *Ego sum panis*, comes from parts of John 6:51, near the end of Jesus's discourse on the Bread of Life. The first part of this antiphon appears as an optional communion antiphon in the missal for the Twentieth Sunday in Ordinary Time. The second part is an option for the Nineteenth. In the preconciliar office for Corpus Christi, the first two lines served as the versicle for the antiphon after the sixth reading at Matins and as the antiphon for the Benedictus at Lauds. In the revised office for the solemnity of the Most Holy Body and Blood of Christ, the same two lines are the versicle for the responsory after the first reading in the Office of Readings, and again as the Benedictus antiphon at Morning Prayer.

As the minister approaches each sick person, someone may walk ahead, carrying a candle (HC 66, in keeping with the option for having a lighted candle on such an occasion in 19).

[28] Benedictines of Solesmes, eds., *The Liber Usualis* (Tournai and New York: Desclée & Co., 1961), p. 1856.

In many hospitals and nursing homes, the fire code forbids such an activity. The suggestion honors the previous rubrics, which had the faithful carry candles or torches to accompany the priest in procession to the sick.[29]

The minister begins the dialogue, "Behold the Lamb of God," as in the missal (OM 132), addressing a roomful of people or the individual who will receive. They give the customary response, beginning "Lord, I am not worthy," and receive in the usual way (HC 66).

The minister says the concluding prayer, either the one from the rite for an individual or one of the alternatives suggested there (HC 62). This concludes the service wherever the minister has gone—back to the original chapel or church, or in the last room (67).

This ritual makes accommodations for the practical difficulties of conducting an integral prayer service in disparate locations. Although not an ideal situation for conducting a liturgy, it provides communion to those experiencing a time of great physical need.

Viaticum

The Church instructs those aware of their impending death to receive communion under the form of Viaticum (canon 921 §1). When the pastor is not available, any ordinary or extraordinary minister of Holy Communion has a duty to administer the sacrament under this form, and must inform the pastor afterwards (canon 911 §1).

The minister wears appropriate vestments (HC 20). In the past, the priest wore cassock, surplice, and stole, if not also a white cope.[30] A lay minister is to dress respectfully (68).

[29] *Rituale Romanum*, Titulus V, Caput IV:10, p. 162.
[30] *Rituale Romanum*, Titulus V, Caput IV:12, p. 162.

The Introductory Rites

The minister greets the people with a formula such as the words Jesus gave the apostles to use upon entering a house (Luke 10:5). The minister places the Sacrament on a table, allowing time for adoration (HC 68). All these instructions repeat those for any communion to the sick (56).

The minister introduces the ceremony (HC 69). The ritual supplies some words taken from those assigned to a priest (PCS 199, or 103 in the Latin edition), but the minister may use similar words more in keeping with the condition of the sick person. The proposed introduction mentions the strength that comes from Viaticum of the Lord's Body and Blood. The General Introduction to PCS connects this sentiment to John 6:54, where Jesus promises to raise up those who eat his flesh and drink his blood (PCS 26, which is the same number in the Latin edition).

After these words, all pray in silence for a while, a practice not indicated in the parallel ceremony led by a priest (PCS 199, or 103 in the Latin edition). The inclusion of silence here may overly interpret the purpose of this introduction, given that all have just silently adored the Sacrament placed on the table and are about to enter silence to call to mind their sins.

The minister introduces the penitential act (HC 70), which resembles the instructions for the administration of communion outside Mass (28) and for bringing communion to the sick (57).

The Shorter Reading of the Word of God

Someone else present or the minister may read a short passage from Scripture (HC 71). The preference is given to another person, as at Mass, where the proclamation of the readings is not the role of the presider (GIRM 59). The reading is not obligatory, but its inclusion follows the preferences of the Second

Vatican Council to expand the use of Scripture in the Catholic liturgy. The Roman Ritual included no Scripture reading in the administration of Viaticum.

The heading calls this a "shorter" reading, which may lead one to wonder, "shorter than what?" It probably means shorter than the reading in a celebration of the Word of God, as in the administration of communion outside Mass (HC 29). Those readings are themselves short; this is shorter. The options listed are those suggested for communion outside Mass and communion to the sick (44, 58).

A note permits other readings from the rite administered by a priest (PCS 298 or 297, or 247ff. or 153ff. in the Latin edition). These are taken respectively from the lectionary's Masses for the administration of Viaticum (796–800) and for conferring the anointing of the sick (790–95). The second group richly provides dozens of passages, but the first group pertains more directly to Viaticum. Some of these readings appear elsewhere in *Holy Communion and Worship of the Eucharistic Mystery outside Mass*. The list follows:

- 1 Kings 19:4-8 (HC 118)
- 1 Corinthians 11:23-26, where Paul affirms that those who eat and drink the sacred bread and cup proclaim the death of the Lord
- Psalm 23:1-3a, 3b-4, 5, 6 (HC 130, 170)
- Psalm 34:2-3, 4-5, 6-7, 10-11 (see HC 131, 173)
- Psalm 42:2, 3, 5bcd; Psalm 43:3, 4, 5, where the soul thirsts for the living God and longs to see God's face
- Psalm 116:12-13, 15 and 16bc, 17-18, where the believer takes the cup of salvation and calls on the name of the Lord
- John 6:51 (HC 138)

- John 6:54, where Jesus offers eternal life to those who eat his flesh and drink his blood
- John 10:9, where Jesus declares himself the gate through which people enter for salvation
- John 11:25, 14:6 where Jesus calls himself the resurrection and the life, the one through whom people gain access to the Father
- John 6:41-51 (HC 150)
- John 6:51-58 (HC 151).

The passage is kept deliberately brief, given that death could be imminent. It also offers a deep meditation on just a few appropriate words of Sacred Scripture.

The Profession of Baptismal Faith

The minister may invite the sick person to renew his or her profession of baptismal faith (HC 72). This is copied from the occasion when a priest leads the service (PCS 190, or 108 in the Latin edition).

In this poignant moment, the sick person, aware that his or her earthly life is drawing to a close, renews commitment to the core tenets of the belief by which he or she lived. This unique preparation for communion outside Mass goes beyond the weekly recitation of the Creed at Sunday Mass. In question-and-answer format, the individual personalizes the conviction of his or her belief, as happens at an event such as the Easter Vigil, the confirmation of a previously baptized Catholic, or when witnessing a baptism.

The preconciliar rite, which rarely assigned spoken words to the people, had no parallel to this. Its addition shows the attention that the revised liturgy gives to the paschal mystery. The English translation of this formula comes from the one in the Roman Missal for the Easter Vigil.

The renewal is optional, though the rubric does not explain why. Perhaps it takes into consideration a sick person who can no longer engage in conversation, though he or she can still swallow. Best, if possible, is for the family or loved ones to contact the local parish to bring Viaticum before debilitating conditions advance.

Prayer for the Sick Person

The minister leads a litany of intentions for the sick person (HC 73), using the formula from the same ceremony when a priest is presiding (PCS 191, or 109 in the Latin edition). Only the title is different. HC calls this the "Prayer for the Sick Person," but PCS calls it a "Litany." The alternate title in PCS is likely an oversight in the original Latin.

The preconciliar rite again had no parallel for this. One can see the Second Vatican Council's interests in the paschal mystery shining through the petitions. The minister introduces the prayer, inviting all present to call together upon the Lord Jesus Christ. Usually petitions are addressed to God the Father, but in this case, the prayers address the Second Person of the Trinity, fully God and fully human.

The first acknowledges the sacrificial death of the Son. The second recalls his pledge to share eternal life with those who eat his flesh and drink his blood. The third proclaims his invitation to the banquet where there is no more sorrow or separation. Other petitions may be used.

The sick person, if possible, is to join in the responses. In practice, the minister will need to assign the gathered faithful the words of their response, and to cue when to say them. In a different setting, such as Mass and Liturgy of the Hours, the reading of petitions such as these is assigned to a different person, not the minister. Presumably, that could be done here, though the rubric does not say.

Viaticum

The minister introduces the Lord's Prayer with the formula taken from administering communion to the sick (HC 59), the one the priest also uses when administering Viaticum (HC 74; PCS 206, or 110 in the Latin edition). It is simpler than the formula at Mass, though it still recalls that Christ taught his followers to use this prayer. All recite the Lord's Prayer together, a common practice before the reception of communion.

The minister shows the sacrament to those gathered and begins the dialogue, "Behold the Lamb of God" (HC 75). Others may receive communion along with the one who is dying; all who will do so make the response, "Lord, I am not worthy." These are the same procedures when bringing communion to anyone who is sick (60).

Going first to the one who is dying, the minister proclaims the formula, "The Body of Christ" (or: "The Blood of Christ"), depending on the manner of reception. After the sick person responds, "Amen," the minister adds another important declaration about Christ: "May he protect you and lead you to eternal life." The one who is dying answers, "Amen." That added formula constitutes the heart of Viaticum. It is a slightly expanded version of the words that the priest says quietly just before receiving communion every time he celebrates Mass (OM 133). He is to be conscious of his mortality daily. Others receive communion in the usual way (HC 76).

A priest uses the same formulas when he administers Viaticum (PCS 193, or 111–12 in the Latin edition). However, in the preconciliar Roman Ritual, the words were different. In administering the sacrament, the priest addressed the dying person in Latin: "Receive, brother (sister), Viaticum of the Body of our Lord Jesus Christ, who may protect you from the evil enemy and lead you to eternal life. Amen."[31] In the revised

[31] *Rituale Romanum*, Titulus V, Caput IV:19, p. 165.

formula, the mention of the power of evil perhaps seemed unnecessary in light of the conquering power of Jesus Christ and his promise of eternal life to those who are faithful to him. "The existing formula brought out the negative effect of the sacrament, namely, deliverance from sin, but was less clear on the positive effect, namely, the spiritual and even the physical relief of the sick person."[32]

The minister purifies the vessel (HC 77). The instruction repeats the one from offering communion to any of the sick (62), complete with the specific word "purification," even in Latin. In the preconciliar rite, the priest washed his fingers in a vessel of water, saying nothing, and dried his hands with a purificator. When possible, he returned this water to church, pouring it down the sacrarium. If that was not possible, he could throw it into fire.[33] Today the minister puts water in the vessel, drinks the water, and dries the vessel.

Concluding Rites

The minister leads a concluding prayer (HC 78). This is basically the collect from the missal's Mass when administering Viaticum, a prayer that was apparently composed for the revised liturgy after the council, as its further antiquity is unknown. A priest administering Viaticum outside Mass offers the same prayer (PCS 209C, or 114 in the Latin edition). The sole difference between this prayer and the collect is that this version says that God's servant has been strengthened not only with the Body but also with the Blood of Christ. It acknowledges the possibility that the person received Viaticum under the form of wine.

[32] Bugnini, p. 685. See also Paul Turner, "Anointing of the Sick and Justice," in *Sacraments and Justice*, ed. Doris Donnelly (Collegeville, MN: Liturgical Press, 2014), p. 106.

[33] *Rituale Romanum*, Titulus V, Caput IV:22, p. 165.

The minister may use an alternate prayer (HC 223). It asks that the servant just renewed by heavenly food and drink may safely reach God's kingdom of light and life. It is the prayer after communion from the missal's Mass for administering Viaticum. A variation appears as the prayer after communion on the anniversary of one's religious profession, number 13B among the missal's Masses for Various Needs and Occasions. There, the priest prays that the professed brother or sister who has just been refreshed by heavenly food and drink may proceed happily on the journey toward God in the religious community. At Viaticum, a dying person may hear a prayer asking that, having been renewed by heavenly food and drink, he or she may reach the kingdom.

The priest has yet another option (PCS 209B, or 57 in the Latin edition). The equivalent concludes communion to the sick by a lay minister (HC 62), but it is not offered in Viaticum as an alternative. It prays for eternal remedy in both body and soul, so it seems an appropriate sentiment, but it has been omitted here.

The minister's final words of blessing are unique to this service (HC 78). They pray that the Lord may always be with the one who is dying, offering strength and peace. The minister does not sign himself or herself as when concluding communion to the sick under normal circumstances (63), probably because the words are directed to one person and not to all. All may then offer a sign of peace to the one who is dying.

These concluding rites invite those gathered to express hope and compassion to the one who is dying. The lay minister's prayerful demeanor will make this possible.

Various Forms of Worship of the Most Holy Eucharist

The third chapter of HC treats three topics: eucharistic exposition, eucharistic processions, and eucharistic congresses. A brief introduction precedes these subjects.

Worship outside Mass presumes reservation of the Eucharist in a tabernacle. Eucharistic reservation developed more in the West than in the East, and fairly recently in Church history. Originally, the altar designated the sacred space inside a building suitable for the gathering of believers.[1] Only later did the tabernacle fulfill that role.

During the Middle Ages, belief in the enduring eucharistic presence of Christ grew in prominence, as did some devotional practices. The earliest record of adoring the Eucharist exposed in a monstrance is found in the life of St. Dorothy, who, in 1394, made a daily visit to church for this purpose. Eventually, entire religious orders were established around this devotion.[2] Tabernacles moved from sacristies into sanctuaries, and ultimately onto the very altar of sacrifice. This practice especially spread after St. Charles Borromeo promoted it.[3]

Eucharistic devotion rose at a time when eucharistic participation had fallen. The people's role at the Mass had diminished, and very few who attended Mass received communion. Adoring the eucharistic presence of Christ substituted for receiving the Eucharist. The Second Vatican Council reanimated

[1] Martimort III, pp. 246–47.

[2] Martimort III, p. 250; and Foley, pp. 7–8.

[3] Martimort III, pp. 247–49.

the people's full, conscious, active participation in the liturgy, along with its most meaningful manifestation: receiving communion. EM 58 aimed to strike a balance between participating at Mass and observing devotions outside Mass, clarifying the preeminence of the former without losing the value of the latter.[4]

An early draft of HC included a presentation of eucharistic theology. As mentioned earlier, the study group abandoned this section of its own draft because the material would have required various authorities to review. It also seemed unnecessary because the Church already had several documents on this theme. This rejected material provides some historical interest. It presents a path once considered but not taken. The early draft's third chapter on the purpose and rite of adoration in the presence of the sacrament made the following doctrinal points:

> 68. The presence of our Savior in the enduring Sacrament has an essential relationship with the paschal Mystery and, through signs, recalls it to the mind of those who pray with appropriate dispositions in the presence of the Sacred Species.
>
> The paschal Mystery, though, is the Gift of Love, which is verified and handed down to the Church in the life of the Lord by separate ancient ways: in the sacramental action of the Mass, in which is celebrated its Memorial, and under the Sacred Species, which are reserved in churches.
>
> This gift is received by the faithful in a more perfect and complete way in sacramental communion.
>
> This gift in a special respect concerns the Church, indeed the whole human race, inasmuch as eating the one heavenly Bread signifies, foreshadows and produces unity in its own way.
>
> But those who participate in the eucharistic banquet keep the covenant that is renewed in the Mass.
>
> All the enumerated applications of paschal benefit will obtain the fulfillment of perfection in paradise.

[4] Martimort III, p. 249.

Now, though, while the Church is on pilgrimage toward the fatherland, Christ remains in various ways with his beloved spouse and nourishes and sustains her on her earthly journey. Among the different modes of this helpful presence of Christ, the one taking first place is the one to which the faith bears witness under the Sacred Species.

Christ associates the Church with himself in the exercise of his priesthood not only in the celebration of the Memorial, but also in other actions and especially when he joins It together with himself in praise and prayer to the Father.

When the faithful pray with due devotion before the Most Blessed Sacrament, they are then united in a special bond with Christ, who is present under Sacred signs.

In the enduring Sacrament the faithful find the sacramental symbol that not only recalls all the paschal benefits for them, but also earnestly demands the response and participation of their mind, heart and work, and still effectively promotes those by extending, with its divine virtue, the grace of the Sacrifice (see EM 3).

All worship shown to the venerable Sacrament becomes more perfect if it is formed with the aforesaid motives. Then they will more fully be conformed to the meaning of the eucharistic mystery and the purpose for which Christ is present in it and sacramentally acts.

So that these appropriate dispositions of the ones praying may be better defined, it helps now to enumerate a little the same aforementioned purposes through the individual points below.

69. (As the Sacrament is the objective memory of the paschal mystery, it demands a devout recollection of the same by those who are praying.)

Under a wondrous sacrament Christ left us perpetually a Memorial, and one especially of his passion and resurrection, so that the faithful may meditate on the mysteries of the Lord and in a particular way on his death and glorious exaltation, if not also on the entire history of salvation. For all the marvels of the ancient covenant of God reach their summit in the paschal mystery. However, this pertains not only to historical events, but it is commemorated in sacramental action at Mass, though in an enduring sacrament, so that it remains stably as clearly living instruction and continuing in its efficacy (see EM 10).

Therefore the Lamb of God, who handed himself over for us that he might take away our sins and those of the whole world (John 1:29, the formula of communion), and who sits at the right hand of the Father to intercede for us, must be adored. The faithful recall that Christ present in the eucharistic sign is the summation of everything in heaven and on earth (Eph 1:7).[5]

70. (In response to the saving gift there should also be an offering, thanksgiving, and prayer for the salvation of all.)

It is fitting for the Eucharist, as the greatest gift of the Love of Christ for humans, that the faithful, praying before the Most Blessed One, express the desires of their offering to Christ. With Christ they offer their whole life to the Father in the Holy Spirit (EM 50).

Similarly the Christian faithful, contemplating the gift of divine generosity, may return gratitude; indeed, in their heart, they may desire to spend their whole life, under the guidance of the Holy Spirit, in thanksgiving (EM 38), ever grateful for the Bread from heaven, in which, under the light of the word of sacramental institution, the whole economy of salvation is revealed to human beings, and they find all the benefits of God toward humans as if this were their synthesis. For it is the most marvelous among the marvels of God.

Christ achieved redemption on the cross and ever extends this in the Mass, handing himself over for the forgiveness of sins and for the life of the world. Therefore the faithful are inspired toward prayer and common work for this purpose, that the reign of God may come, and their brothers and sisters may be saved.

71. (A stirring sign toward Sacramental Communion and toward preparing for it.)

By regarding the Species, the faithful stir up their desires for eating the Bread of angels. Spending time in the presence of

[5] *Sic*. The reference is to Ephesians 1:10.

Christ the Lord, they enjoy his intimacy and familiarity and pour out their heart before him.

From a marvelous exchange and union with Christ they draw an increase of faith, hope, charity, and nourish the right dispositions in which, by an equal devotion, they may celebrate the memorial of the Lord and frequently receive that Bread given to us by the Father (EM 50).

Spiritually they eat the divine banquet, uniting themselves to Christ the Lord with a living faith, which works through love (EM 38).

72. (The internal connection to the extent of which the Sacrament is a sign of unity and a bond of charity.)

The sacrament of unity summons Christians again to preserving unity in the bond of charity. No prayer can be more suitable to this mystery than that which brings unity and is directed toward obtaining it.

The eucharistic sign suggests to the faithful that they live according to the Spirit of Christ, who is the source of the unity of his Body. For this reason St. Augustine says about those receiving Holy Communion, that they may also rely on spiritual communion and prayer before the enduring Sacrament.

"The faithful come to know the body of Christ if they do not neglect to be the body of Christ. . . . Do you want therefore to also live by the Spirit of Christ? Let it be in the body of Christ. . . . You cannot live as the body of Christ except by the Spirit of Christ. This is how the apostle Paul explained this bread to us: 'Because the loaf of bread is one, we, though many, are one body' (1 Cor 10:17).

"O Sacrament of devotion! O sign of unity, O bond of charity! The one who wants to live . . . possesses that by which one may live. . . . Let one not shrink from joining the members, let one not be a decaying member that deserves to be cut off, let one not be turned away from that which restores one's complexion: let one be beautiful, let one be fit, let one be healthy, let one cling to the body, let one live for God by God; now one labors on earth that one may reign later in heaven" (St. Augustine, *On the Gospel of John*, tractate XXVI, c. VI, 13; PL 35, 1612-1613).

The Eucharist also, as an enduring sacrament, signifies the unity of all believers (EM 8), and it also brings about charity through faith in Christ.

The faithful who are stirred up by the Symbol of unity and affected by sorrow concerning the divisions of Christians, pour out prayers before God the Father that all the disciples of Christ may become one body according to his true intention (1 Cor 10:17), "linked by the very bonds by which he wishes it to be constituted" (EM 8, "Mysterium Fidei," AAS 57, 1965, 773).

73. (The pattern of a new covenant that inspires faithfulness.)

Let the faithful think of the eucharistic sacrament as a sign of the Lord's covenant and faithfulness. Let them be moved toward trust in the fulfillment of his promises and inspired to keep the agreements that especially by baptism or religious profession they have sealed with their Lord. Similarly let them devote themselves to God and ever renew their covenant with him (EM 36). Let them strive to keep themselves in the behavior and life that they believe to be present in the eucharistic celebration. Let them regard and cling to it as an example and consolation, remedy, strength and help against temptations and adversities.

With devotion toward the Most Blessed Sacrament may the attention of the faithful be so nourished that they strive to accomplish good works pleasing to God and rightly performed, to become zealous for the Church, to do what they learned from the Master, and to advance in devotion, so that the world may be imbued with the Christian spirit, and also present themselves as witnesses of Christ before all, even in the middle of human affairs (see EM 13).

74. (The Sacrament may stand out as a sign and pledge of eternal glory for heavenly desires.)

Prayer before the Living Medicine of immortality and the Pledge of future glory may take place in view of eternal life and be nourished by the expectation of the blessed hope and coming of the Savior (EM 8, eucharistic prayer).[6]

[6] *Sic.* The reference is to the embolism after the Lord's Prayer in the Order of Mass.

> 75. (The sign of Christ praying and praising, and associating himself with humans.)
>
> Christ, who went about doing good and healing all, remains in the Sacrament as medicine to cure the infirmities of human beings. He intercedes to the Father on behalf of all. He is also the victim of expiation. Faith necessarily associates those who adore in his presence with the prayer of Christ for peace, the needs of the Church, and of all brothers and sisters, and of the world.
>
> Christ seeks true adorers who may praise God the Father through him and with him and in him. Those who pray are able to achieve this in a special way in the presence of this Sacrament.[7]

The next drafts completely removed these doctrinal points and presented new introductions to the entire work and to this section.[8] Braga's revision remained substantially the same as the introduction that stands at the head of this chapter in the final version of HC. Its main points are summarized below.

The Mass is the source and summit of the Christian life, so eucharistic devotion both at Mass and outside it, in public and in private, is most appropriate. The times of the liturgical year provide a framework for uniting eucharistic worship with the Mass (HC 79).

The Constitution on the Sacred Liturgy affirmed the centrality of the Mass in Christian life, using the memorable descriptors "source" and "summit." "The liturgy is the summit toward which the activity of the church is directed; it is also the source from which all its power flows" (SC 10).[9] EM 58 applied this to frame eucharistic devotion within the purpose of the Mass.

The idea of harmonizing adoration with the liturgical seasons also appeared in EM 58, which in turn referenced the Constitution on the Sacred Liturgy (SC 13). Without giving details,

[7] Schema 401, pp. 17–21.

[8] Schema 403 (1–3), pp. 20–21; and Schema 405 (1–3), pp. 20–21.

[9] *Vatican Council II*, p. 122.

these documents express the hope that popular devotions taking place within the liturgical year will hold the seasons in mind. This could be accomplished through appropriate Scripture readings, decorations, prayers, and music, for example.

In its presentation on the preconciliar practice of Forty Hours Devotion, the Roman Ritual had included a series of prayers pertaining to the seasons of the year. The priest selected the appropriate prayer for the period from Advent to Christmas, from Christmas to the Purification of the Lord, from the Purification to Easter and from after Easter Time to Advent, and during Easter Time.[10]

The introduction to chapter III further connects eucharistic sacrifice and adoration. The faithful who adore should recall the sacrifice that tends toward both sacramental and spiritual communion (HC 80). A similar point appears in the theological section of the early draft.[11] In 1947, *Mediator Dei* favorably cited the Council of Trent's encouragement that the faithful attending Mass receive sacramental communion, not just a spiritual one.[12] In the case of adoration, the faithful may experience a spiritual communion as they worship the Sacrament while recalling the sacrifice.

Making a spiritual communion became popular during the height of the COVID-19 pandemic, when churches among other buildings were closed to public gatherings. Many Catholics began watching Mass livestreamed onto their screens at home. As the priest received the host and drank from the cup, many were invited to pray an act of spiritual communion, such as one composed by St. Alphonsus Liguori, for the benefit of the faithful who for whatever reason could not receive.[13]

[10] *Rituale Romanum*, Titulus V, Caput VII, pp. 184–185.

[11] Schema 401 (69), p. 18.

[12] *Mediator Dei* 118, citing Trent Sess. 22, c. 6.

[13] For versions by Alphonsus Liguori and Cardinal Rafael Merry del Val, see https://www.vaticannews.va/en/prayers/the-spiritual-communion.html. For a more contemporary version by Sr. Judith Kubicki, CSSF, of Fordham University, see https://www.oldstpats.org/spiritualcommunionprayer.html.

Those spending time in adoration would fruitfully reflect on the sacrifices they make in their own lives. By recalling their own self-offering in the Mass, they meditate on the offering of Christ, the fruits of which are evident in the reserved Sacrament.

The faithful who adore are drawn to participate in the paschal mystery, especially at the Mass, and to respond in gratitude for Christ, who continues to pour his divine life into his body, the Church. Given their intimate familiarity with Christ, they pray for themselves and for their loved ones, and for the peace and salvation of the world. In faith, hope, and love, they prepare themselves to participate more devoutly at Mass, especially by receiving communion (HC 80).

As the priestly people, those who adore offer prayers. This practice too prepares them to participate more fully at Mass. They may bring to adoration specific prayers for their own needs and those of their families. They may also be aware of parts of the world experiencing civil unrest, and they are to bring the intention of peace for them into their prayer.

The faithful should therefore include adoration in their spiritual exercises, and pastors should encourage them to do so (HC 80). This also recalls a point from the earlier draft, that the Lamb of God must be worshiped.[14]

While adoring, the faithful should recall the covenant with God, celebrated in the Eucharist, which commands moral behavior in their life. They live on the strength of this heavenly food, performing good works, pleasing God, imbuing the world with the Christian spirit, and becoming a witness to Christ in human affairs (HC 81).

This final section of the introduction also draws from the early draft.[15] It in turn relies on points from EM 13, inspired by several of the documents of the Second Vatican Council.

[14] Schema 401 (69), p. 18.
[15] Schema 401 (73), p. 20.

Eucharistic adoration appeals to the interior life. It gives adorers an experience of silence, away from screens and conversations, in which they can enjoy the attractive intimacy of prayer with the Sacrament of the Body of Christ exposed for their adoration. The final part of the introduction to chapter III cautions them that this is not enough. The spiritual growth that they obtain from the interior life drives them into the world to live in purity, to bear witness to Christ, and to fill the earth with his spirit.

Exposition of the Most Blessed Sacrament

Introduction

Before presenting the order of service for exposition of the Blessed Sacrament, HC offers another introduction to underscore certain points. These again concern the theological relationship between exposition and Mass, a theme already explored in numbers 1 through 4, and 80, and which the ritual deems important enough to restate. This introduction also takes up practical considerations relating to the ceremony and the minister.

Christ is truly present in the Eucharist, and union with him reaches its summit in communion, but exposition in a ciborium or in a monstrance encourages faith and devotion. Preparations should therefore avoid anything that obscures the desire of Christ to be close to his people as food, medicine, and comfort (HC 82). These points echo those made in EM 60, and they reappear at the head of the section on exposition and Benediction in the Ceremonial of Bishops (1102). Worship of the Blessed Sacrament is important, but it does not substitute for nor rank higher than participation in communion at Mass.

While exposition takes place, Mass is forbidden in the same part of the church. The Mass includes more perfectly the interior communion also achieved in exposition. If exposition extends over a period of days, it is interrupted for the celebration of Mass, or Mass is celebrated in a separate space. In that case, those who adore do not leave their post in order to attend part of the Mass (HC 83). This number comes from the late drafts and refers to EM 61.[16] The Code of Canon Law repeats the prohibition of Mass during adoration (941 §2).

To explain the reasons for keeping Mass separate from exposition, HC 83 refers back to 6. The earlier number details the ways in which Christ is really present in the Mass, and it concludes that Mass may not be celebrated on an altar with a tabernacle where the Blessed Sacrament is reserved. The presence of Christ is the fruit of the consecration and needs to appear as such. The later number shows that in addition to making clear the results of the consecration, the separation of practices also shows that interior communion is more perfectly achieved within sacramental communion at Mass.

These opening paragraphs come directly from the later drafts. However, the drafts did not refer back to HC 6 as 83 does. Furthermore, they included one phrase that has been removed. In referring to the internal benefits of adoration, the drafts said that exposition aims to lead the faithful toward interior communion "and therefore is not lacking such sustenance."[17] The removal of that phrase avoids any confusion about the superiority of the fruits of communion over those of adoration.

An early draft showed the difference between celebrating Mass and celebrating the Liturgy of the Hours in the presence of the sacrament:

> Exposition lasting throughout the same time would obscure the importance and meaning of the Mass in the mind of the faithful. . . .
>
> The Liturgy of the Hours, on the other hand, is not at all forbidden to be celebrated in the presence of the Most

[16] Schema 403 (5), p. 21; and Schema 405 (5), p. 21.

[17] Schema 403 (4–5), p. 21; and Schema 405 (4–5), p. 21.

> Blessed One. For it concerns especially the psalms and formulas that are either the voice of the Church to Christ, or the voice of Christ to the Father, or the voice of the Church with Christ to the Father, that speak about Christ or excellently extol or accord with the meditation of Christ.[18]

The introduction also considers points to be observed in arranging exposition (HC 84–85). In the past, a person showed reverence to the exposed Blessed Sacrament by genuflecting on both knees—that is kneeling down for a brief moment and then rising again. The decision to require only genuflection on one knee (84), which the missal describes as bending the right knee to the ground (GIRM 274), goes unexplained. However, the Blessed Sacrament deserves adoration and does not increase in holiness when it is exposed. The same reverence fittingly applies. The introduction takes this instruction word for word from the late drafts.[19] It reappears in the Ceremonial of Bishops (1103).

The subsequent rubrics make no reference to the posture of the faithful during the time of adoration. The minister kneels while incensing the sacrament (HC 97), but the faithful receive no instructions regarding posture. A single genuflection implies that after showing reverence, they may assume whatever posture seems appropriate—sitting, standing, or kneeling—as they may do before a tabernacle with the Blessed Sacrament enclosed.

Exposition may be arranged either with a monstrance or a ciborium (HC 85). In the case of the ciborium, which is less common, the covered vessel is placed on the altar for the adoration of the faithful, and two candles are lighted. A monstrance displays a consecrated host through the glass of a more ornate vessel, and four or six candles are to be lighted. The

[18] Schema 401 (88), p. 24.
[19] Schema 403 (14), p. 24; and Schema 405 (14), p. 24.

number of candles shows the relationship between exposition and the Mass, for the missal requires two candles—or four or six—especially for a Sunday, a day of greater solemnity (GIRM 117). Incense is always used when the host is on view in a monstrance. Here and elsewhere the ritual assumes that exposition takes place within a liturgy, not as an exercise of private devotion.

This changes the requirements from the late drafts, which recommended but did not require incense, and presented the options in reverse order. "If exposition takes place with a ciborium, at least two candles may be lit; or four or six—that is to say as many as are lit at Mass—if exposition takes place with a monstrance. Incense is used if appropriate especially when exposition takes place with a monstrance."[20] The use of incense "if appropriate" is mentioned in the Order of Mass at the entrance, the gospel, and the preparation of the gifts (1, 15, 27). The final version of the rubrics for exposition remove the qualifier and require incense with exposition in a monstrance.

When a bishop presides, incense is to be prepared in the sacristy beforehand (CB 1104b). He will incense the Sacrament accordingly (1109).

The introduction next considers periods of extended exposition (HC 86–88). Calling this "solemn exposition," a term that the Sacred Congregation of Rites preserved (EM 63), it is recommended annually in churches and oratories that reserve the Eucharist, provided that a suitable number of the faithful are present (HC 86). This resembles the preconciliar custom of Forty Hours Devotion before the Blessed Sacrament, but HC no longer names a number of hours. In fact, if it is difficult to have a continuous lengthy period of exposition, it may be interrupted. Opportunities for such adoration will invite the local community to meditate on the eucharistic mystery and to adore the Sacrament more profoundly.

[20] Schema 403 (12), p. 24; and Schema 405 (12), p. 24.

Another reference to this practice appears in the rubrics for exposition (HC 94), which compares the ordinary exposition of the Blessed Sacrament with a "more solemn" one. This implies that any eucharistic exposition is "solemn"; an extended one is more solemn.

This paragraph comes from the late drafts, and it makes a few changes. It adds "oratories" to the places under consideration. It also more strongly urges this practice. The drafts said that annual extended exposition "may take place," but the final version says "it is recommended" that it take place.[21] The drafts also repeated a phrase from EM 63, which says that extended exposition was to take place "with the consent of the local ordinary and according to the law," but those words were removed. Perhaps this intended to encourage local initiative in arranging such a solemn exposition. The Code of Canon Law repeats these changes from the final version of this paragraph (942).

The local ordinary may allow an even longer period of exposition. This applies to places where faithful pilgrims assemble in greater numbers, creating a more serious and general need (HC 87).

The drafts included another qualifier about the protracted time, "which may be strictly continuous." Although it appeared in EM 64, the final version of HC removed it. This acknowledges the difficulty in establishing continuous periods of lengthy expositions and more directly permits their interruption for a time.

HC 88 tells how to manage those periods of interruption. In such cases, the Sacrament is placed in the tabernacle at previously scheduled times. Such reposition may take place up to twice a day, such as midday and night. The same paragraph describes a "simpler" reposition in which a priest or deacon wearing a stole over an alb or over a surplice and cassock

[21] Schema 403 (6), p. 22; and Schema 405 (6), p. 22.

adores the Sacrament briefly, prays with the faithful, and places the Sacrament in the tabernacle. When worshipers can reconvene, the Sacrament may be exposed in a similar way. By restricting this to twice a day, the process retains the sense of a single lengthy exposition.

The last drafts provided similar guidance, relying on more details from EM 65. They defined the simpler way of reposition as one without singing. For the minister, they mention only a priest, not alternatively a deacon, dressed in surplice and stole. They called for his private adoration, but not yet any prayer with the faithful. They note that after placing the Sacrament back on the altar, he would adore for a while and then withdraw. These details were removed from the final version of HC, but EM 65 still appears in a footnote.[22]

An early draft, though, made other provisions that the later drafts and final book abandoned:

> In the absence of a group, individuals praying before the Most Blessed One may also find useful nourishment in that practice in which, without solemn exposition, the tabernacle may be opened, or, if this has been fashioned of glass or crystal, a canopy or curtain may be removed from it, so that the eucharistic vessel, and perhaps also the species if they are displayed in a clear vessel or on a paten, may be viewed.
>
> This accomplishes then another form of showing, which is distinguished from solemn exposition intended for the common worship of a gathered congregation.
>
> In religious communities, a male or female lay superior, or others designated by them, may also open the door of the tabernacle to start continuous adoration and enact it by the rotation by different members of the community. Similarly, it belongs to them afterwards, when adoration has been completed, to close the tabernacle.

[22] Schema 403 (8), p. 22; and Schema 405 (8), p. 22.

> These same persons may start solemn exposition whenever the whole community has gathered for adoration at the same time. The same persons enact reposition without benediction when this is over, as indicated below.[23]

Permission for a glass tabernacle has been completely removed (HC 10). Exposition takes place on the altar (93), but 91, without further explanation, lists opening the tabernacle as one method of conducting exposition. Perhaps this alludes to churches where the tabernacle remained on the altar in the sanctuary, also addressed in 93. The same early draft offered additional advice:

> If the community after solemn exposition has to depart so that only one or a few remain to extend continuous adoration, some time of common adoration may be inserted, done with songs, prayers and silence. Then a priest or someone else reposes the Sacrament, intending to expose it again later when, for example, the community regathers at Vespers to pray before the Most Blessed One. Private adoration may be continued at the place of reservation, the Sacrament having been shown as indicated in n. 82 above.
>
> Nevertheless, where the custom prevails of extending exposition in the manner described above for solemn exposition even when only one or a few members of the community take turns in adoration, the community may keep the custom if this is judged appropriate for a reasonable cause.[24]

In the end, HC promotes the practice of perpetual adoration. However, it envisions reposition of the Sacrament at intervals during a lengthy exposition when it is difficult for a sufficient number of people to sustain it.

[23] Schema 401 (82–83), p. 22.
[24] Schema 401 (86), p. 23.

When a parish provides a prolonged period of adoration, HC 88 applies. If an insufficient number of people has agreed to be present, a minister is to repose the sacrament up to twice a day at previously announced times. Careful planning avoids a circumstance in which one or two people in adoration discover that no one has arrived to take their place. There is no provision for them to cover an exposed monstrance with a cloth and leave it unattended, or to press a button for its automated retraction. A properly designated minister of communion is to repose the Sacrament and close the tabernacle door. The parish is to ensure that the Blessed Sacrament receives proper respect, and that ministers fulfill their duties.

An early draft noted that, if the rite has been interrupted for reposition, Benediction still takes place. However, it is done after the final period of adoration.[25]

More common are brief expositions of the Blessed Sacrament (HC 89). Even here, time is set aside for readings from Scripture, hymns, prayers, and silent prayer. Presumably this is also true when a bishop presides, though such details about pious exercises during the period of exposition are missing from CB 1115. Exposition only for giving Benediction is prohibited. This section repeats material from EM 66 and from the drafts, which also specifically placed responsibility on the ordinary that such expositions always and everywhere happen with due reverence. They also prohibited exposing the Blessed Sacrament at the end of Mass just to give Benediction,[26] a practice that would confuse the purpose of communion at Mass. In HC 89, all such extremely brief expositions are prohibited—not just those at the end of Mass. This implies that the first purpose of exposition is adoration of Christ, and that Benediction is a supplementary benefit for the people.

[25] Schema 401 (97), p. 27.

[26] Schema 403 (9), p. 22; and Schema 405 (9), p. 22.

Certain religious communities retain perpetual or extended adoration before the Blessed Sacrament as part of their charism (HC 90). HC asks that their practice align with the liturgical norms. When the whole community is gathered, periods of adoration are to include readings from Scripture, song, and silence to nurture the spiritual life of the community and to develop its unity. HC commends the practice in which one or two members of the community take turns adoring the sacrament. They adore in the name of the community and of the Church.

HC 90 offers the only reference in the book to the minimal number of people who may adore the exposed sacrament at one time. It permits a single member of a religious community to maintain continuous adoration until another member arrives. Presumably, this applies to parochial circumstances outside religious communities as well. However, such individual adoration takes place within a larger liturgy at which more were present at the beginning and will be at the end. Throughout, HC envisions multiple people present to fulfill roles such as server, reader, and musician, and to lead a gathered assembly.

These provisions expand those found in the drafts.[27] The last draft adduced material from EM 50, which encourages all the faithful, not just religious, to worship Christ the Lord according to their proper way of life. That reference has been removed from HC 90, presumably because it pertains to more than religious. In 1973, the Congregation for Religious, aware of this forthcoming order of service, asked the Vatican's Secretariat of State that the final form not give the impression "that community adoration is preferred to private, thus creating uneasiness and division within religious institutes whose

[27] Schema 403 (10), p. 23; and Schema 405 (10), p. 23. This is a rare instance where 405 rearranged some of the material from 403 and added the citation from the end of EM 50.

constitutions call for continuous adoration of the Blessed Sacrament in their churches or chapels."[28] This accounts for the strong language near the end of this number, which highly commends the practice of one or two members taking turns in adoration.

The final section of the introduction treats the minister who exposes the Eucharist for adoration. The ordinary minister is a priest or deacon, who blesses the faithful with the Sacrament before returning it to the tabernacle. The drafts too restricted the blessing to the ordained minister, though the earlier one placed the information within the rubrics of the ritual.[29]

If no ordained minister is present, an instituted acolyte, a deputed lay minister of Holy Communion, or someone appointed by the bishop may expose the Sacrament for public adoration. These permissions are repeated in canon 943. Lay ministers have three options for exposing the Sacrament: opening the tabernacle door, placing a closed ciborium on the altar, or exposing a host in a monstrance. At the end of the period of adoration they replace the Sacrament in the tabernacle and close the door (HC 91).

One draft explained the reason for allowing lay ministers to assist:

> The purpose of the new norm is, at the intervention of the diocesan bishop, to provide an advantage for communities and pious societies dedicated to perpetual adoration, who encounter difficulties due to the absence of a priest or a deacon who may provide for the exposition or reposition of the Most Blessed One. Concessions as an indult in this matter are already given by this Sacred Congregation. The new norm would be a broader concession,

[28] Bugnini, p, 662, fn. 76, citing a letter summarizing the issue, sent from the Secretariat to the Sacred Congregation for Divine Worship on July 18, 1973. See also his fn. 77.

[29] Schema 401 (90), p. 25; Schema 403 (11), p. 23; and Schema 405 (11), p. 23.

> which entrusts the matter to the bishop, for the same reason concerning a minister for distributing communion. However, such ministers of exposition will not be able to bestow the blessing.[30]

In fact, two of the drafts specifically mentioned the intent to provide such ministers for religious communities. One limited the lay minister to one who was already permitted to distribute communion, while the subsequent draft changed it to one who has the faculty for this particular task.[31] This paragraph was removed, presumably because the permission applies both within and without religious communities.

The same two drafts more explicitly offered the option of adoration before an opened tabernacle door. Lay ministers could open the door at the beginning of adoration and close it at the end, and, if appropriate, place a ciborium (though not a monstrance) on the altar.[32] HC 91 retained the option of adoration before an open tabernacle door and added the possibility of exposing a host in a monstrance.

For vesture, a priest or deacon wears a white stole over an alb or over a cassock and surplice. In the United States, if it is the local custom, either minister may also wear a cope, a rare permission for a deacon. Lay ministers wear whatever is appropriate for this ministry in their region as approved by the ordinary. When a priest or deacon imparts a blessing with the monstrance at the end of adoration, he wears a white cope and humeral veil. If he gives a blessing with the ciborium (a practice not much observed), he wears a humeral veil, not the cope (HC 92).

The late drafts had worded this differently. A cleric was to wear an alb or cassock and surplice, and a deacon or priest

[30] Schema 403, p. 4.

[31] Schema 403 (11), p. 23; and Schema 405 (11), p. 23, another rare instance where these schemata differ.

[32] Schema 403 (11), p. 23; and Schema 405 (11), p. 23.

would add a white stole. (In the past, a man became a cleric with tonsure even before receiving minor orders, but now he becomes a cleric only with ordination to the diaconate.) Others wore something appropriate to their ministry. According to the late drafts, to give the blessing at the end of exposition with the monstrance, a priest or deacon wore a cope.[33]

When a bishop presides, he too wears an alb and stole, but also a pectoral cross and cope of "appropriate color," which presumably could be white, seasonal, or pertinent to the liturgical day. As a rule he wears a miter and carries the pastoral staff. When deacons assist the bishop, they wear the dalmatic or deacon's stole. If priests assist, they wear copes (CB 1106 and 1115).

The Order of Eucharistic Exposition and Benediction

The ceremony transpires in four parts: exposition, adoration, benediction, and reposition. An early draft envisioned the same structure with these descriptions: "Exposition of the Sacrament," "Period of adoration before the exposed Most Blessed One, enacted by a community gathered at the same time," "Benediction with the Sacrament made with the formulas and sign of the cross," and "Reposition of the Sacrament."[34] The same draft entitled the ceremony "The Rite of Adoration," but the late drafts changed the title to "The Order of Exposition of the Most Blessed Sacrament."[35] HC 93 expanded this to "The Order of Eucharistic Exposition and Benediction," even though benediction is omitted when a lay minister presides.

Exposition begins when the people have gathered (HC 93). As noted above in the order for distributing communion out-

[33] Schema 403 (13), p. 24; and Schema 405 (13), p. 24.

[34] Schema 401 (76), p. 21.

[35] Schema 403 (15), p. 24; and Schema 405 (15), p. 24.

side Mass (27), this seemingly unnecessary requirement endearingly mimics the expression found at the beginning of the rubrics in the Order of Mass. It stresses that the order of service does not belong to the priest alone. The People of God celebrate the liturgies of the Church. After they have gathered, the ceremony begins.

An early draft encouraged exposition on the very altar where Mass is celebrated. "Thus the connection between the worship of the Species and the paschal sacrifice may even be more openly recognized by the place."[36]

The top of the altar, the mensa, is to be covered with a cloth (HC 93), presumably white. Although many parishes set out a corporal on the altar, it is not mentioned here: only a cloth. However, the Ceremonial of Bishops, citing this very number, interprets it to permit a corporal if circumstances suggest (1108). If exposition with a monstrance is over a longer period of time, a throne may be prepared, though not too elevated or distant, as indicated in EM 62. The drafts, citing the same source, made the same point.[37]

To begin, a song may be sung, and the minister approaches the altar. The passive voice in HC 93 renders unclear who sings the song, though it seems to imply that all the people sing it. An early draft specified that "the faithful may offer a song in honor of the Lord."[38] The other drafts included the song for those occasions when exposition does not follow Mass.[39] They recommended specific titles, but permitted "other hymns existing in the Liturgy of the Hours that celebrate the paschal mystery of Christ."[40]

[36] Schema 401 (78), p. 22.

[37] Schema 401 (77), p. 21; Schema 403 (12), p. 24; and Schema 405 (12), p. 24.

[38] Schema 401 (78), p. 22.

[39] Schema 403 (24), p. 16; and Schema 405 (24), p. 16.

[40] Schema 403, p. 30; and Schema 405, p. 30.

When exposition takes place apart from Mass, this is the traditional moment when the people have sung the eucharistic hymn *O salutaris hostia*. The words are the final two strophes of the longer hymn *Verbum supernum*, which remains recommended for Morning Prayer in the celebration of the Liturgy of the Hours for the solemnity of the Most Holy Body and Blood of Christ, formerly Corpus Christi. The opening words are well translated as "O Victim, bringing saving grace," but the appearance of the word *hostia* for "Victim" may have influenced the popular usage of the hymn when a consecrated host was set into a monstrance and on display for the adoration of the people. HC presents the entire hymn in its fourth chapter (194). Although it never recommends the usage of the final two verses at the beginning of exposition, the custom is so prevalent that the English translation in the United States has added it to 93 as one option both in English and in Latin.

The same chapter provides other alternatives for this eucharistic hymn, or for the one to be sung later, just before benediction (HC 97). The suggested list comes from the Roman Ritual's collection of hymns for eucharistic processions,[41] marking only a few changes. Many come from the office of Corpus Christi, attributed to St. Thomas Aquinas. *Pange lingua*, "Sing, My Tongue, the Hidden Mystery," described below at the conclusion of adoration, occupies the first place (192).

Sacris sollemniis, "Let our Joys Magnify Sacred Solemnities" (HC 193), was the hymn at Matins in the preconciliar feast of Corpus Christi. It remains as the hymn for the office of readings on the solemnity of the Most Holy Body and Blood of Christ. It recounts the institution of the Eucharist at the Last Supper, recalls the charge Christ gave priests to offer the sacrifice, and marvels at the bread of angels shared among the lowly. The Belgian composer César Franck set to music the final two verses, beginning with the words *Panis angelicus*, and

[41] *Rituale Romanum*, Titulus X, Caput V:4, pp. 804–810.

they remain a standard among solo and choral music. The image alludes to Psalm 78:25, which calls the manna that miraculously fell from the desert sky the bread of angels.

Verbum supernum, "The Word Proceeding from on High" (HC 194), is well known for its final two verses mentioned above, *O salutaris hostia*. The complete hymn was composed for Lauds on Corpus Christi and remains at Morning Prayer for the solemnity of the Most Holy Body and Blood of Christ. The hymn professes the coming of the Word made flesh, who gave himself as food to his disciples, died to ransom sinners, and reigns as their reward.

The Roman Ritual's list of hymns for eucharistic processions next included *Salutis humanæ Sator*, the hymn at the preconciliar Lauds and second Vespers for the feast of the Ascension of the Lord. The postconciliar Liturgy of the Hours replaced it with *Iesu nostra redemptio*, "O Jesus, Our Redeeming Lord," a curated text of the same hymn, which it uses for both first and second Vespers for the solemnity of the Ascension of the Lord. The same replacement appears in the list of eucharistic hymns (HC 195). Its words are addressed to Jesus, who suffered for sinners, ransomed them, and sits at God's right hand, while asking him for the same pardon over sinners today.

Æterne rex altissime, "Eternal King and God Most High" (HC 196), also serves in the Liturgy of the Hours at the office of readings on the solemnity of the Ascension of the Lord. It was the last of the hymns from the Roman Ritual's eucharistic processions. The postconciliar editions use a more recently curated version of the Latin. The words address Christ, the Redeemer King, sitting on the Father's right, ruling over all, whose flesh overcame the sins of the flesh. It prays for pardon and redemption.

Lauda Sion, "Laud, O Zion" (HC 197), is the sequence for the solemnity of the Most Holy Body and Blood of Christ, and the full text can be found in the lectionary. Now optional on that day, it was obligatory at the preconciliar Mass of Corpus

Christi. It calls upon the new people of Zion to praise Christ, especially for the life-giving bread shared at the Last Supper. The celebration on this day commemorates that sacrament as the communion that unifies those who partake. This lengthy poem is also attributed to Aquinas.

Adoro devote, "Hidden Here Before Me" (HC 198), is a recension of a hymn that Pope Pius V inserted into the front of the Roman Missal in 1570 as one of the prayers of thanksgiving for a priest to say after Mass. It has been attributed to Aquinas and has been used in celebrations of Benediction.[42] Several variants of this Latin hymn are in existence, but the study group chose for the first time the one from the critical edition of André Wilmart.[43] The words express the believer's experience beholding the real presence of Christ in the Eucharist.

The last hymn, *Ubi caritas*, "Where True Charity" (HC 199), comes from the Roman Missal's washing of the feet during the Holy Thursday evening Mass of the Lord's Supper. It calls on the members of the community, gathered in the love of Christ, to love God and to love one another. The revisers included in HC the words reconstructed by Karl Strecker.[44] The opening line, familiar to many as "*Ubi caritas et amor*," has been edited as "*Ubi caritas est vera*," that is, from "Where charity and love are" to "Where true charity is." The same hymn is recommended for the Blessing of a Religious House in the US edition of the *Book of Blessings* (720).

Presumably, the reverences appropriate at the beginning of Mass apply here: if the tabernacle is in the sanctuary, the minister in procession genuflects; if not, the same minister makes

[42] Dom Matthew Britt, OSB, ed., *The Hymns of the Breviary and Missal* (New York: Benziger Brothers, 1952), p. 189.

[43] Bugnini, p. 663, n. 79, citing *Auteurs spirituels du moyen âge latin* (Paris, 1932), pp. 361–414.

[44] Bugnini, p. 663, n. 79, citing *Monumenta Germanie Historica (Poetae latini Aevi Karolingi), IV, II, 1, 526–29,* and E. Franceschini, "Dov'è carità e amore qui c'è Dio," in *L'Osservatore Romano*, June 1, 1972.

a profound bow to the altar (GIRM 274 and 275b). When a bishop presides, this is clear: he puts aside his pastoral staff and miter, usually into the hands of another minister, and either bows to the altar or genuflects to the Blessed Sacrament if it is reserved in the sanctuary (CB 1107).

The ritual again does not describe the posture of the assembly. However, when a bishop presides, after making his reverence and before a deacon or priest brings the Sacrament to the altar, he kneels (CB 1107 and 1115). Presumably, the faithful, who have stood for the hymn and the procession, kneel with the presider.

The minister approaches the tabernacle. At the time this ritual book was composed, the location of tabernacles was in flux. Previously, they had all been located on the altar where the priest celebrated Mass. However, after the council, this practice was criticized: "because of the sign, it is more in keeping with the nature of the celebration that the Eucharistic presence of Christ, which is the fruit of the consecration and should be seen as such, should not be on the altar from the very beginning of Mass through the reservation of the sacred species in the tabernacle" (EM 55). This principle subsequently entered the missal (GIRM 315). Nonetheless, there are some churches where this practice persists. When a bishop presides at such an altar, the Blessed Sacrament is to be transferred somewhere else before he begins the Mass (CB 49). If exposition takes place at such an altar, then the minister need not wear a humeral veil to expose the Sacrament for adoration. In more normal situations, the minister does wear the veil, and servers or members of the faithful accompany the minister bearing lighted candles (HC 93). The late drafts made similar points,[45] though the use of the humeral veil was added to the final version. Even if the walking distance between the tabernacle and the altar is short, the minister wears the veil for that procession.

[45] Schema 403 (16), p. 24; and Schema 405 (16), p. 24.

HC 93 does not distinguish between an ordained and a lay minister. It implies that even a lay minister who approaches a tabernacle apart from the altar wears a humeral veil to transport the vessel. The garment pertains more to the Sacrament than to the minister.

If exposition is in the ciborium, the minister places the vessel directly upon the altar cloth. If exposition is in a monstrance, the minister first prepares the vessel. The ritual book does not explain how. In many churches and oratories, a previously consecrated host is kept in a glass lunette secured inside a repository within the tabernacle. One minister carries an empty monstrance to the altar and sets it sideways on the altar cloth. The minister who carries the repository to the altar opens it there, withdraws the lunette, opens the back of the monstrance, slides the lunette inside, closes the monstrance, and turns that vessel to face the people.

An early draft provided other somewhat surprising alternatives that the final version did not approve. "The Species may be exposed either in a ciborium with a lid and preferably having been removed, or in a monstrance with glass and a lunette; or in a paten similar to the one used at Mass. If the Species of wine are reserved, these also may be exposed in the chalice."[46] Not only did the final version of HC remove these options, but the Church teaches that consecrated wine is not to be reserved in the tabernacle,[47] probably out of a concern that the substance of the wine not turn sour.

When a bishop presides, a deacon wears the humeral veil to carry the Sacrament from the place of reservation. The deacon prepares the monstrance and sets it on the altar. The ritual does not say if he prepares the monstrance apart from the altar or on it, but customarily the action takes place on the altar, perhaps out of convenience. In the rare instance when the

[46] Schema 401 (79), p. 22.

[47] *Norms for the Distribution and Reception of Holy Communion*, par. 54.

Sacrament is to be exposed on the same altar where the tabernacle is located, the deacon does not wear the veil. After exposition, the deacon genuflects and takes his place beside the bishop, presumably kneeling (CB 1108 and 1115).

Upon exposing the Blessed Sacrament in a monstrance, the minister incenses it (HC 93). Incense is optional for exposition in a ciborium (CB 1115). Even the drafts called for incense "especially if exposition takes place with a monstrance."[48] When a bishop presides, the deacon holds the boat, a censer-bearer holds the censer, and the bishop adds incense to it from the boat and blesses it (CB 1109). Logically, ministers would assist other presiders in a similar way. In like instances the missal specifies that a priest says nothing as he blesses (GIRM 277), implying that he only moves his hand in the form of a cross over the billowing smoke. By tradition, a presiding lay minister would not bless the incense. According to the missal, a minister takes the censer, bows, incenses the Blessed Sacrament with three swings, and bows again (GIRM 277). After bowing the second time, a bishop returns the censer to the deacon (CB 1109), and similarly a priest would pass the censer to the minister who handed it to him. If exposition is continued for a longer time, the minister may either withdraw, as the drafts permitted,[49] or remain in the sanctuary, a bishop either at his chair or at another appropriate place (HC 93 and CB 1110).

Periods of "more solemn" and extended exposition begin after the distribution of communion at Mass (HC 94). Catholics have customarily referred to this ceremony as "solemn exposition," but the revised ritual avoids the expression (apart from HC 86), perhaps because it seems tautologous. Any exposition is solemn. An extended one is more solemn.

[48] Schema 403 (16), p. 24; and Schema 405 (16), p. 24.

[49] Schema 403 (16), p. 24; and Schema 405 (16), p. 24.

In this case, the priest who presides consecrates an extra host at the Mass, which is placed in the monstrance after the communion of the faithful. Presumably the priest himself places the lunette inside the monstrance, as he is to set the monstrance on the altar for the adoration of the people. However, a deacon may prepare the monstrance when a bishop presides (CB 1108), so presumably he could do the same for a priest.

Mass ends with the prayer after communion, and the priest omits the concluding rites, as indicated in EM 60. If appropriate, he sets the monstrance on a throne to incense it (HC 94). When a bishop presides for exposition at the end of Mass, he too incenses the sacrament (CB 1105). This paragraph comes directly from the late drafts, which cite EM 58 as the source,[50] from a section that pertains to maintaining the relationship between the liturgy and non-liturgical celebrations.

EM 60 explains that beginning a prolonged exposition with the Mass shows the relationship between these two actions. Even the preconciliar Clementine Instruction recommended that Forty Hours Devotion begin with celebration of the votive Mass of the Most Blessed Sacrament.[51]

The drafts similarly proposed beginning exposition with Mass, a practice with which the revisers would have been familiar:

> When exposition takes place immediately after Mass, the Species consecrated in it are exposed so that the worship of the enduring Sacrament may appear to draw its origin from the Mass and be worshiped as an extension of the grace of the sacrifice.
>
> Exposition may then take place immediately after the prayer that follows communion.
>
> When the rite of exposition has been completed, and the incensation perhaps performed, a time of adoration in silence may take place. Some song may follow the si-

[50] Schema 403 (15), p. 24; and Schema 405 (15), p. 24.

[51] *Rituale Romanum*, Titulus V, Caput VII:1, p. 174.

> lence. Then, after the prayer after communion has been said, the priest departs, having omitted the rite of blessing and dismissal of the Mass.
>
> Similarly, if the exposition takes place immediately after Mass, it belongs to the priest celebrant to expose the Sacrament for public worship so that a better connection with the Mass may even be apparent in the minister.[52]

HC 94 ultimately moved the exposition from the initially recommended moment following the prayer after communion to the moment preceding it. This apparently strengthened the connection between the eucharistic sacrifice and worship of the eucharist, while incorporating the prayer after communion within the period of adoration.

Adoration of the Blessed Sacrament may be enhanced with prayers, songs, readings, homilies or exhortations, and silence to help the faithful devote themselves to Christ and to appreciate the eucharistic mystery (HC 95). In practice, many periods of adoration take place in complete silence. This provides a countercultural time when people, away from other distractions, may center themselves for prayer. However, the use of vocal means of adoration emphasizes the communal dimension of the experience.

These recommendations come from EM 62. They are repeated in CB 1111 for occasions when the bishop presides. The first draft offered a scope of opportunities, without removing the option for silence:

> Worship of the community gathered for adoration is also carried out through a sacred reading, which ought to be chiefly biblical, though other spiritual reading may also be from the Fathers or even from other writers who are able to generate piety or devotion. Readings of the Mass or from the Liturgy of the Hours readily provide this useful nourishment. There may also be, if appropriate,

[52] Schema 401 (80–81), p. 22.

> responsorial songs or other songs, psalms, hymns or other texts in use. A homily or another exhortation, as those in the group or the appendices suggest, may take place. Prayers of intercession set forth in the missal or the Liturgy of the Hours or elsewhere, or composed for this purpose, may laudably be recited. All formulas of this kind should always respect the current liturgical time or celebration proper to the day (EM 58). Moreover, all formulas are to be made so that they are directed to God.[53]

HC 95 adopts paragraphs from the later drafts.[54] These refined the more Christological purpose of the period of adoration and explicitly added the option for silence.

If adoration takes place following the communion rite of the Mass, the first hymn to be sung is often *O salutaris hostia*, as already noted in HC 93. Nonetheless, some other appropriate hymn may be sung.

Worshipers may pray some of the Liturgy of the Hours during the period of adoration, especially Morning and Evening Prayer. This extends the praise and thanksgiving to God beyond the Mass and into the various hours of the day. The prayers of the Church are directed to Christ and through him to the Father (HC 96). These suggestions come from the drafts, which permitted them even for shorter periods of exposition.[55]

The same practice is recommended when a bishop presides (CB 1111). In the United States, the English translation of HC 96 specifies that these principal hours end without the blessing that usually concludes them. Instead, after the prayer of the day, the presider adds the formula, "May the Lord bless us . . ." as used in individual recitation of these hours or when a layperson presides. However, if benediction follows immediately, even that formula is omitted. In this way, benediction

[53] Schema 401 (87), p. 23.

[54] Schema 403 (17), p. 25; and Schema 405 (17), p. 25.

[55] Schema 403 (18), p. 25; and Schema 405 (18), p. 25.

with the Blessed Sacrament more fittingly concludes the entire period of adoration.

In the Roman Ritual, a series of adoration exercises filled the practice of Forty Hours Devotion. The ceremony began with a solemn votive Mass of the Most Blessed Sacrament. A procession with the Sacrament then formed while the hymn *Pange lingua* was sung, except for its final verses, the *Tantum ergo*, which were sung at the conclusion of the procession when the celebrant set the Blessed Sacrament upon a throne and incensed it. There followed the litany of the saints, Psalm 70, dialogic verses sung with cantors, and a prayer appropriate to the occasion or time of year. On the third day the priest again celebrated the votive Mass of the Most Blessed Sacrament. The litany, psalm, and prayers of the first day were repeated. The celebrant incensed the Sacrament and led a procession through the church during the first verses of the *Pange lingua*, which were repeated if necessary. When the priest returned to the altar, the cantors intoned the *Tantum ergo*, and the celebrant again incensed the Blessed Sacrament. At this point the cantors added the dialogue *Panem de cælo*, and the celebrant stood to sing prayers. He then blessed the people with the Sacrament and reposed the host in the tabernacle.[56]

The Roman Ritual provided a set of orations that changed for the occasion or time of year. They can still be found in the postconciliar liturgy. The first option, a generic choice, appears throughout this ritual book (HC 38, 50, 98), the aforementioned collect for the Mass on the solemnity of the Most Holy Body and Blood of Christ. The Roman Ritual also used it for communion of the sick.[57] The Roman Ritual's oration for the time from Advent up to Christmas is now the missal's first collect for the Common of the Blessed Virgin Mary in Advent. The

[56] *Rituale Romanum*, Titulus V, Caput VII: *Litaniæ, Preces et Orationes quæ dicuntur in Exposiciones et Reposiciones SS.MI Sacramenti pro Oratione XL Horarum*, pp. 174–187.

[57] *Rituale Romanum*, Titulus V, Caput IV: 24, p. 167.

oration used from Christmas through the Purification (February 2) is the missal's first collect for the Common of the Blessed Virgin Mary in Christmas Time, and it is repeated as the collect for the solemnity of Mary the Mother of God (January 1). The oration for the period between the Purification until Easter, and after Easter Time until the beginning of Advent, reappears as the missal's first collect for the Common of the Blessed Virgin Mary in Ordinary Time. The Roman Ritual's oration for Easter Time is the collect for the Common of the Blessed Virgin Mary during the same period.

The Roman Ritual provided other orations. The one for the pope did not carry into the postconciliar missal. However, the missal does include three other collects in its second Mass for Various Needs and Occasions: "For the Pope." The Ritual's oration for the Church is now the first option for concluding the sample universal prayer in appendix V of the Roman Missal. The Ritual's final prayer, a general plea for God's mercy, does not appear in the missal. An oration such as these could still be included among the various public elements in the period of adoration.

The third major part of the service is benediction with the Blessed Sacrament, as noted even in EM 62. A priest or deacon approaches the altar, genuflects, and then kneels (HC 97). When a bishop presides, he too goes to the altar, hands his pastoral staff to a minister, genuflects, and then kneels (CB 1112–13). In some instances, the bishop may be arriving at exposition for the first time, especially in the case of a prolonged exposition where another priest has presided over the services thus far. In those cases, the bishop enters with pastoral staff and miter, but sets them aside, genuflecting and kneeling before the sacrament, presumably for a short time of adoration (CB 1107). The basic instructions also appeared in the late drafts.[58]

[58] Schema 403 (25), p. 19; and Schema 405 (25), p. 19.

A eucharistic hymn is sung (HC 97), although, in contrast to the previous practice, *Tantum ergo* is not required. Those final verses of *Pange lingua* remain the common eucharistic hymn to conclude the period of adoration. However, even EM 62 permitted another eucharistic hymn to replace it. Commentary in one of the drafts explicitly listed this as one change: "In place of the one hymn *Tantum ergo*, the singing of another hymn or antiphon or responsory about the Most Blessed Sacrament is permitted (n. 19). Texts not exclusive of others, especially when it comes to songs in the vernacular language, are indicated in Chapter III."[59] Those are now in chapter IV (HC 192–99) as described above. The complete text of *Pange lingua* is the first of them (HC 192). In the United States, both the English and the Latin words of the final two verses are copied into HC 97. Singing *Tantum ergo* connects worshipers to ages past and to other Catholics around the world.

In the preconciliar office, *Pange lingua* served as the hymn for first solemn Vespers on the feast of Corpus Christi. Its words set the context for adoring the sacrament: it is the sacramental Body of Christ, who was born of the Virgin and who gave his Body and Blood as food and drink. The Latin edition of the postconciliar Liturgy of the Hours still uses the hymn for first Vespers on the solemnity of the Body and Blood of Our Lord Jesus Christ. In the Roman Ritual, *Tantum ergo* concluded the period of adoration for Forty Hours Devotion.[60] The Roman Missal also recommends all of *Pange lingua* for the procession that concludes the Holy Thursday evening Mass of the Lord's Supper, and it reserves the final two verses, the *Tantum ergo*, for the incensation of the Sacrament after it has been placed in the tabernacle.

The fourth chapter also provides a set of responsories (HC 204–9). According to commentary in a late draft, these offer an

[59] Schema 403 (3b and 1), p. 4.

[60] *Rituale Romanum*, Titulus V, Caput VII:II4, p. 187.

alternative to *Tantum ergo* at the end of the period of adoration.[61] The texts "were taken either from liturgical books in force or from some tradition of particular churches,"[62] but the specific sources are not cited. Their purpose is unexplained in the final version of HC, even though these are exactly the responsories that the late drafts included as alternatives to the hymn referenced at what is now HC 97.[63]

The first, "While they were at supper" (HC 204), comes from the preconciliar office of Corpus Christi, where it followed the fourth lesson at Matins. The words of the refrain (Matt 26:26 and Mark 14:22), describing Jesus's actions at the Last Supper, also inspired part of the missal's Eucharistic Prayer IV. The versicle is from Job 31:31, where people wonder who will give the flesh that satisfies.

The second, "I am the bread of life" (HC 205), followed the sixth lesson at the same office, where it also incorporated the doxology, "Glory be to the Father, and to the Son, and to the Holy Spirit." The biblical source is John 6:48-51. Parts of this responsory appear in the missal as the second recommended communion antiphon for the Twentieth Sunday in Ordinary Time, and the communion antiphon found in the second set of prayers "For One Deceased Person" among the Various Commemorations in the Masses for the Dead.

The third, "Recognize in the bread" (HC 206), comes from Augustine's Sermon 228B on the sacraments at Easter Time. It alludes to 1 Corinthians 6:15, where Paul reminds his readers that they are members of Christ. It professes faith in the sacramental Body of Christ while affirming its unifying benefits.

[61] Schema 403, p. 4.

[62] Schema 403, p. 5.

[63] Schema 403, p. 31; and Schema 405, p. 31.

The fourth, "Though many" (HC 207), was used in some traditions for Matins or Vespers on Corpus Christi.[64] The first part (1 Cor 10:17) reappears in the missal as the communion antiphon for the Twenty-Seventh Sunday in Ordinary Time. The versicle comes from Psalm 68:11. It professes the unity of those who share the one bread and one chalice, and the kindness of God who provides a place where all may dwell as one.

The fifth, "A certain man" (HC 208), expands the antiphon from the preconciliar Lauds on the Sunday within the octave of Corpus Christi. It draws from Luke 14:16-17, the parable of the man who sent his servant to invite guests to his great feast, and adds a versicle taken from Proverbs 9:5, where Wisdom invites all to eat and drink the prepared bread and wine.

The last, "The living Father sent me" (HC 209), comes from Matins in the preconciliar office for Corpus Christi, the responsory following the eighth lesson, which also included the doxology. It combines John 6:57, where Jesus promises life to those who eat him, with Sirach 15:3, which declares that the Lord feeds with the bread of life and of understanding.

A skilled chant choir would find musical settings of many of these in Latin among various collections. These many options invite new musical settings in the vernacular languages.

During the hymn or antiphon, the minister incenses the Sacrament if exposition has taken place with a monstrance (HC 97). Although only a priest or deacon approaches the altar in preparation for the blessing, a minister who presides for the service in his absence could still incense the Sacrament. The Roman Ritual had called for this incensation to take place during the last verse of *Tantum ergo*.[65] The rubric has not carried over into the revised ritual, which therefore allows incensation at any time during the singing. An early draft called for incense

[64] https://cantusdatabase.org/chant/525949, and https://cantusdatabase.org/chant/681254.

[65] *Rituale Romanum*, Titulus V, Caput VII:II:4, p. 187.

"if it was used in the Mass of the day,"[66] but now it is expected any time there is exposition with a monstrance.

The bishops of the United States did not receive their request that, after this incensation, a verse and response may be added ("You have given them bread from heaven. Having all sweetness within it"), affixing an alleluia to the end of each phrase during Easter Time. They had also requested the same dialogue in Latin, beginning with *Panem de cælo*, as many know the words in the original language. It had been included in countless celebrations of Benediction of the Blessed Sacrament in the United States in the decades after the Council, even though the postconciliar HC did not have it. The dialogue does appear in the postconciliar *Graduale Romanum* after *Tantum ergo* at celebrations of Benediction, but that volume was published nearly at the same time as the revised ritual. Perhaps the editors of the *Graduale* did not realize that the dialogue had been removed. Its omission here validates the work of the members of the study group who revised HC.[67]

An early draft offered *Panem de cælo* with alternative versicles, as mentioned above. One was based on the third verse of Psalm 128, another came from an antiphon at Matins for Corpus Christi, and another citing 1 Corinthians 5:7-8 was proposed for Easter Time.[68] All of these reappeared in the later drafts along with two more.[69] One of these came from Psalm 107:8-9: "Let them thank the Lord for his mercy, for he fills the hungry with good things." The other used Psalm 111:4-5: "The Lord has made a memorial of his wonders. He has given food to those who fear him." All these versicles were removed from the final version of HC.

[66] Schema 401 (91), p. 25.

[67] Virgilio Noé, "Commento," *Notitiae* 86 (1973), p. 332.

[68] Schema 401 (91), p. 25; see p. 63 above.

[69] Schema 403 (20), pp. 25 and 32; and Schema 405 (20), pp. 25 and 32.

The minister stands and invites all to pray (HC 98). As elsewhere, the rubrics do not assign posture to the people. In practice, many remain kneeling; however, at Mass, at the words "Let us pray," the people stand for the oration. Even when exposition takes place at Mass, the people stand for the prayer after communion in the presence of the Blessed Sacrament.

After some silence, the minister offers a prayer (HC 98). The ritual does not indicate which direction the minister faces. At Mass, such orations are usually said facing the people; however, the minister may feel drawn to face the Blessed Sacrament—even though the prayer is addressed to the Father, not to Christ. When a bishop presides, he holds his hands outstretched (CB 1113). Presumably, a priest or deacon would do the same. A deacon extends his hands for prayer when presiding at a wedding, for example (Order of Celebrating Matrimony 89), so the same could apply here when he presides. There is no indication that a lay presider would extend hands for this prayer.

The recommended prayer is the familiar collect from the solemnity of the Most Holy Body and Blood of Christ. The Roman Ritual had set this same prayer as the first for a similar moment near the end of Forty Hours Devotion. On the devotion's third day, it introduced a repetition of the orations from adoration on the first day.[70] The same prayer appeared at this point of exposition in all the drafts of HC.[71]

All the drafts offered alternative prayers, and these formed the basis for the ones that remain, most of which were drawn from the Paris Processional of 1690.[72] An early draft recommended the collect that remains in the missal for the votive

[70] *Rituale Romanum*, Titulus V, Caput VII, II:1-2, pp. 186–187.

[71] Schema 401 (92), p. 25; Schema 403 (20), p. 25; and Schema 405 (20), p. 25.

[72] Bugnini, p. 663, fn. 79.

Mass of the Most Holy Eucharist,[73] but the other drafts set it aside, possibly for the sake of variety: it already appears as an option for the prayer after communion in the rite of administering Holy Communion outside Mass (HC 210).

The first option, "Lord God, we believe" (HC 224), appeared in all the drafts, the earliest of which calls it the first option from the Paris Processional.[74] It expresses belief that the historical Jesus Christ is present in the Sacrament and prays for eternal salvation from this divine font. The imagery alludes to Isaiah 12:3.

The second, "Grant us, we pray" (HC 225), appeared in all the drafts, the earliest of which called it the third option from the Paris Processional.[75] It asks for the grace to offer worthy praises to the Lamb slain and hidden in the Sacrament in order to contemplate him in glory. It alludes to Revelation 5:12.

The third, "O God, who have given" (HC 226), appeared in all the drafts, the earliest of which called it the fourth option from the Paris Processional, while the others noted that the words have been adapted from that source.[76] It prays that by the power of the true bread from heaven the faithful may live in God and rise on the last day. The prayer alludes to John 6:32.

The fourth, "Enlighten our hearts" (HC 227), appeared in all the drafts, the earliest of which called it the sixth option from the Paris Processional.[77] It prays for the light of faith and the fire of love to adore in spirit and in truth. The prayer alludes to the alleluia verse before the gospel on Pentecost Sunday, a popular prayer to the Holy Spirit. It also references Jesus's conversation with the Samaritan woman in John 4:23-24.

[73] Schema 401 (92), p. 25.

[74] Schema 401 (92), p. 25; Schema 403, p. 34; and Schema 405, p. 34.

[75] Schema 401 (92), p. 25; Schema 403, p. 34; and Schema 405, p. 34.

[76] Schema 401 (92), p. 25; Schema 403, p. 34; and Schema 405, p. 34. Bugnini also notes the slight adaptation, p. 663, fn. 79.

[77] Schema 401 (92), p. 25; Schema 403, p. 35; and Schema 405, p. 35.

The fifth, "May the Sacraments" (HC 228), found in the late drafts, replaces a suggestion from the early draft, the tenth option from the Paris Processional, with another unnumbered option from the same source.[78] This one prays that the sacraments may fill hearts with divine sweetness, making them long for the riches of the kingdom.

The last, "O God, who by the Paschal Mystery" (HC 229), found in the late drafts, replaces another suggestion from the early draft, the twelfth option from the Paris Processional, with a prayer adapted from the missal.[79] The source is the collect from the votive Mass of the Most Precious Blood of Our Lord Jesus Christ. The prayer here changes the opening words from the missal, "by the Precious Blood of your Only Begotten Son," to "by the Paschal Mystery of Christ." This achieves the practical effect of repurposing a prayer to be used in adoration of the Body of Christ, while setting into a foremost position one of the main themes of the Second Vatican Council, the paschal mystery.

After the prayer, a priest or deacon who presides prepares to administer the blessing with the Blessed Sacrament (HC 99). A lay minister may not do so (HC 91). The priest or deacon puts on a humeral veil. In practice, a server usually helps him by standing behind him and holding it aloft over his shoulders. The priest or deacon drapes the ends around his shoulder and fastens the veil in front with its morse or clasp. Some humeral veils have pockets at the ends, into which the minister inserts his hands. Even when using a veil without pockets, he is to raise the vessel with some cloth protecting it from contact with his bare hands during the blessing. The Ceremonial states this more explicitly when a bishop presides (CB 1114). A deacon

[78] Schema 401 (92), p. 25; Schema 403, p. 35; and Schema 405, p. 35.

[79] Schema 401 (92), p. 25; Schema 403, p. 35; and Schema 405, p. 35. Bugnini erroneously notes that HC 228 is the prayer adapted from the missal, p. 663, fn. 79.

may help the bishop, though the Ceremonial does not explain how; perhaps he guides the ends of the veil toward the vessel. Approaching the monstrance or ciborium, the priest or deacon genuflects before it, stands, takes the vessel in hand, and makes the sign of the cross over the people, saying nothing. The Ceremonial does not offer the bishop the option of blessing with the ciborium.

HC is silent about the posture of the people. Traditionally they kneel. However, at Mass, Morning and Evening Prayer, and other rituals, the people stand for blessings. Sometimes the deacon commands them to bow. If they have stood for the prayer, they could stand for this blessing. However, in practice, people usually kneel.

The rubrics specify that the minister says nothing during the blessing. In the Roman Ritual he gave the blessing "in the customary way."[80] HC 99 clarifies that this does not mean the way a priest gives the blessing at the end of Mass, naming the Holy Trinity.

An early draft did provide words for a blessing, admitting that the formulas still needed revision. The priest or deacon, after the prayer following *Tantum ergo* or another hymn, turned to the people. At the time, those preparing the draft were most familiar with the preconciliar practice of exposition on an altar fixed to the wall. The draft therefore instructed the priest to face the people without losing his view of the Sacrament. As the priest or deacon stood in this position, the draft provided these or similar words before blessing with the monstrance:

> May almighty God, whose Only Begotten Son, on the night before he suffered, left a memorial of his Passion under a marvelous Sacrament, bless you, and may he raise your intention to the heights.
>
> ℟. **Amen.**

[80] *Rituale Romanum,* Titulus V, Caput VII:II:5, p. 187.

> And may he who is the Bread of Angels, made to be the food of the faithful (and living creatures) in the manger of the Church, make you taste in the present the sweetness of eternal joys, and lead you in the future to a participation in the highest rewards.
>
> ℟. **Amen.**
>
> Concerning the one whose flesh in truth is wondrously consumed and whose blood is drunk under the species of bread and wine, may his flesh cleanse and his blood wash away your sins that you committed in flesh and blood.[81]

A subsequent draft also promoted words of blessing before or even with the movement of the monstrance:

> In place of the prayer that may be offered by the priest or deacon after the hymn, an opportunity is provided for a formula of some blessing, like the solemn blessing at the end of Mass.
>
> The sign of the cross with the Sacrament over the people, besides being given in silence as is now the custom, may be given with some formula of blessing wherever it is customary or was in the old tradition (see the Ambrosian Rite, and also other particular Rituals, especially of the dioceses of Germany).[82]

The late drafts recommended a spoken blessing by the priest before giving benediction with the vessel, offering two examples. Again, he was instructed not to turn his back on the Sacrament while facing the people:

> May the almighty and merciful Lord, who accomplished your salvation in the paschal mystery of Christ, enrich with heavenly blessings you who venerate this Sacrament with devout minds.
>
> ℟. **Amen.**

[81] Schema 401 (94), p. 26.

[82] Schema 403 (3b and 2–3, referencing 21 and 22), p. 4.

And may you who in faith proclaim the death and resurrection of Christ, discover a bond of unity and peace in this sacrament of mercy.

℟. **Amen.**

So that, remaining in thanksgiving, you may bear the fruits of good works in communion with Christ and reveal his wonders to the world for its salvation.

℟. **Amen.**

Or:

May the almighty and merciful Lord, whose Only Begotten Son, on the night before he suffered, left a memorial of his passion under a marvelous sacrament, bless you.

℟. **Amen.**

And may the One who feeds you with the nourishment of his Body and Blood both provide helps for salvation and make you sharers of his divine nature.

℟. **Amen.**

And, through him who is the bread coming down from heaven, may he make you taste in the present the sweetness of eternal joys, and lead you in the future to a share in the highest rewards.[83]

Concerns about the priest not turning his back on the Blessed Sacrament did not enter the final version of HC. Perhaps this relates to the growing custom of the priest facing the people during Mass in a church where the tabernacle may have been situated behind him, demonstrating the unimportance of these concerns. Some Catholics, however, notably in the Latino community, still practice a related devotion. Some of them, if they leave the presence of the exposed Blessed Sacrament during a period of adoration, walk backwards toward the door, so as not to turn their backs on the Sacrament. The rubrics neither expect nor encourage this practice.

[83] Schema 403 (21), p. 26; and Schema 405 (21), p. 26.

The drafts implied or clearly stated that the minister approached the altar without a genuflection.[84] However, HC 99 inserted one before he gives the blessing with the Sacrament.

Although the late drafts envisioned that the priest or deacon would bless the people with the monstrance or ciborium "saying nothing," they permitted this alternative: "Wherever it is in force, the practice of making this sign of the cross by offering some formula of blessing may nonetheless be maintained."[85] Permission for such spoken words of blessing was removed from the final version of HC 99.[86]

An early draft explained the meaning of Benediction and its restriction to an ordained minister:

> To understand better the meaning of eucharistic Benediction, one must pay attention well to the Church's ministry of imparting favors. For Benediction is a rite that the Church exercises through the hands of a priest or deacon.
>
> In the Eucharist, Christ is plainly the perpetual font of blessing for the Christian people and for the entire world. All good giving and every perfect gift comes down from the Father of lights (Jas 1:17). However, in all favors to be obtained, Christ is the sole and unique Mediator between God and humans. He gave himself as a ransom for all (1 Tim 2:5-6). God has blessed us in Christ with every spiritual blessing in the heavens (Eph 1:3). Through the rite of Benediction the Church in no way diminishes this living font of universal and permanent blessing that is always present in the Eucharist, but rather extols it by drawing from the fonts of the Savior [Is 12:3].[87]

[84] Schema 401 (95), p. 26; Schema 403 (22), p. 26; and Schema 405 (22), p. 26.

[85] Schema 403 (22), p. 26; and Schema 405 (22), p. 26.

[86] Schema 401 (95), p. 26; Schema 403 (22), p. 26; and Schema 405 (22), p. 26.

[87] Schema 401 (89), p. 24.

The rubrics make no mention of swinging incense or ringing bells at this time. In the United States, the bishops requested and received permission for a minister to swing incense during the blessing as an option. Presumably, bells are not to be rung.

A bishop traditionally makes the sign of the cross with his hand three times (CB 169), but the number is missing in these instructions (1114). Apparently he makes the sign with the monstrance only once.

The divine praises, a mainstay in the celebration of Benediction, never appeared in the drafts or the final version of HC. Even the Roman Ritual's description for the close of Forty Hours Devotion has the priest repose the sacrament into the tabernacle immediately after the blessing, without any further words or ceremonies.[88] Still, in the United States, Catholics widely associate them with the concluding parts of Benediction.

They come from various sources. Several popes have embellished the original list of eight praises likely composed in Italian by Jesuit Father Luigi Felici in 1797 in reparation for blasphemies against the divine name.

Blessed be God.

Blessed be his Holy Name.

Blessed be Jesus Christ, true God and true man.

Blessed be the name of Jesus.

Blessed be his Most Sacred Heart (added by Leo XIII in 1897, two years before he asked for the whole world to be consecrated to the Sacred Heart of Jesus).

Blessed be his Most Precious Blood (added by St John XXIII in 1960).

Blessed be Jesus in the Most Holy Sacrament of the altar.

Blessed be the Holy Spirit the Paraclete (added by Blessed Paul VI in 1964).

Blessed be the great Mother of God, Mary Most Holy.

[88] *Rituale Romanum*, Titulus V, Caput VI:5.

Blessed be her holy and Immaculate Conception (added by Blessed Pius IX in 1851, three years before the proclamation of the dogma of the Immaculate Conception in 1854).

Blessed be her glorious Assumption (added by Pius XII in 1952, two years after the proclamation of the dogma).

Blessed be the name of Mary, Virgin and Mother.

Blessed be St Joseph, her most chaste spouse (added by Pope Benedict XV in 1921 [a year after his motu proprio *Bonum Sane*, promoting devotion to the same saint]).

Blessed be God in his Angels and in his Saints.[89]

These ultimately found a home in the moments near the end of Benediction. The bishops of the United States requested and received the option of inserting them after the blessing and before reposition, giving formal permission to a practice that was already widespread.

The last of the four parts of the ceremony is reposition of the Blessed Sacrament. After the blessing, a priest or deacon places the Sacrament in the tabernacle and genuflects, presumably before closing the door (HC 100). The people may say some acclamation. The minister leaves. If a lay minister has presided, he or she logically reposes the Sacrament without giving the blessing. This was clearer in the early draft.[90]

When a bishop presides, a deacon takes the monstrance from his hands and places it on the altar. Both of them genuflect. The bishop removes his humeral veil and kneels while the deacon transfers the Blessed Sacrament to the place of reservation. He does so "reverently." Does that mean he wears the humeral veil that the bishop just removed? Presumably so, because he wore it to transfer the sacrament from the tabernacle to the altar in CB 1108. He genuflects before closing the door of the tabernacle (CB 1114).

[89] John Flader, "What Is the Origin of Divine Praises We Say in Benediction?," *The Catholic Weekly*, July 8, 2016, https://www.catholicweekly.com.au/what-is-the-origin-of-divine-praises-we-say-in-benediction/.

[90] Schema 401 (96), p. 26.

The early draft specified that the minister made no genuflection after Benediction when picking up the vessel just before its reposition. The genuflection was to be made after the Sacrament was placed in the tabernacle and before closing the door.[91]

The same draft permitted the faithful to sing a hymn or psalm during the reposition. "It is fitting that the hymn be some praise or thanksgiving for the blessings of God."[92] The bishops of the United States received approval for their request that at the conclusion of the liturgy, the people have the option either to make an acclamation or to sing a hymn. This honors the widespread custom of concluding Benediction with the popular hymn based on the *Te Deum*, "Holy God, We Praise Thy Name." Otherwise, that hymn would be missing from the official liturgy of Benediction.

Unlike the conclusion of Mass or the principal offices of the Liturgy of the Hours, there is no formula of dismissal. The faithful simply leave at their discretion. However, the early draft envisioned one. The minister said, "Go in peace," and the people responded, "Thanks be to God." The minister made the appropriate reverence and then departed.[93] The dismissal does not appear in the later drafts or in HC 100. Perhaps this demonstrates the devotional nature of this service. Unlike Mass, its focus is more introspective than evangelical.

Eucharistic Processions

Devotion to the real presence of Christ cascades into streets in carefully organized eucharistic processions. Several paragraphs articulate the main goals and express various concerns (HC 101–8). The topic had been broached in EM 59, which

[91] Schema 401 (96), p. 26.
[92] Schema 401 (96), p. 26.
[93] Schema 401 (97), p. 27.

provides the source for the drafts[94] and for HC 101. Processions celebrate the faith of the people, even as they bear witness to it in public.

In preparing these paragraphs, one draft issued some cautions: "Keeping in mind the quite diverse social conditions and those of a practical order, which today may limit or prohibit the possibility of this procession, only general indications can be given, which will have to be integrated with legitimate local traditions."[95]

The diocesan bishop is to judge the appropriateness of such processions to ensure that they transpire with dignity without harming proper reverence of the Sacrament (HC 101). He may permit additional processions in large cities, but he should decide on the advisability of their time, place, and plan (HC 102, CB 386). This may include restricting certain motorized conveyances that lend insufficient dignity to the Sacrament or processional routes where devotion could become compromised. Canon law affirms the bishop's authority over regulations for these processions for the purpose of participation and dignity (944). Therefore, a parish wishing to add a eucharistic procession to an observance such as the solemnity of the Most Holy Body and Blood of Christ is to submit their plans for the bishop's approval.

The practice continues one that faith-filled ancestors have long observed. Clergy lead the procession. The faithful walk in an orderly manner from one sacred place to another, giving voice to hymns and prayers. Some processions have had a specific purpose, such as giving thanks for God's favor or imploring God's aid. Pastors are to give the faithful proper preparation (CB 1093).[96] An early draft noted:

[94] Schema 403 (1), p. 27; and Schema 405 (1), p. 27.

[95] Schema 403, p. 4.

[96] The Ceremonial cites as its source the Roman Ritual, Titulus X, Caput I:1.

> Through a procession, all the citizens offer an impressive image that they are and that they see themselves as a pilgrim church, which, under the sacred reign of Christ the Head, is directed toward the heavenly city shining with his light. The faithful signal that they are in the rank of people who "pass from this pilgrim table to the banquet of our heavenly homeland" (see the Roman Missal, [prayer after communion,] on the Solemnity of All Saints).[97]

One of the primary occasions for eucharistic processions is the solemnity of the Most Holy Body and Blood of Christ (HC 102, CB 385 and 1095), when even the missal encourages adoration (GIRM 3 and the note that concludes the presider's texts for the solemnity.) The event expresses the common faith and adoration of the people.

The origins of this solemnity go back to the visions of Belgian Sister Juliana of Liège in 1208, which prompted her bishop to promote its inclusion in the calendar. St. Thomas Aquinas is believed to have composed the office, and eucharistic processions started in Cologne from 1274 to 1279. By 1316, Pope John XXII included processions in the celebration of Corpus Christi.[98]

An early draft promoted the custom:

> It is fitting that the Solemnity of the Body and Blood of Christ be celebrated everywhere with the special splendor of songs and ceremonies, and embellished in the Mass and the Liturgy of the Hours. A more perfect participation in the memorial of the Lord should be encouraged through the communion of all the faithful people, even those not present, especially the sick in homes or hospitals, applying also the permissions noted elsewhere in this instruction.[99]

[97] Schema 401 (105), p. 29.
[98] Lane, pp. 8–9; and Foley, p. 20.
[99] Schema 401 (99), p. 28.

Another draft suggested, "In places, though, where there are several parishes, it is fitting to have one procession for all, in witness of the unity in worshiping this marvelous Sacrament."[100] This suggestion did not survive the subsequent draft.

Where a procession is difficult, a public celebration may be held in the cathedral or other suitable places (HC 102). The drafts introduced this idea,[101] probably out of a concern that processions were hard—or even illegal—to organize in some cities.

The procession ideally begins after Mass and features a host consecrated at that Mass (HC 103, CB 387 and 1097). Specifically for the solemnity of the Most Holy Body and Blood of Christ, the missal too prefers that the host carried in procession be consecrated at the Mass immediately preceding it. Even the preconciliar rubrics called for the priest to consecrate two hosts at this Mass—one for his communion, and the other for adoration.[102] The monstrance with the host is placed on the altar, the priest says the prayer after communion, and the concluding rites are omitted (CB 387). However, HC 103 and the missal also note that a public procession may follow a lengthy period of adoration after a Mass. This information carries over what the drafts had provided.[103]

When a bishop presides, after the communion of the faithful, a deacon sets the monstrance on the altar and places within it a host that the bishop had consecrated at that Mass. The bishop and his assisting deacons genuflect, and he returns to the chair, where he offers the prayer after communion (CB 389). No humeral veil is involved because there is no procession: the host is moving directly from the altar into the monstrance resting there. These details are missing from HC 105, but presumably a presiding priest could enlist the assistance of a deacon to set

[100] Schema 403 (2), p. 27.

[101] Schema 403 (2), p. 27; and Schema 405 (2), p. 27.

[102] *Rituale Romanum*, Titulus X, Caput V:2.

[103] Schema 403 (3), p. 27; and Schema 405 (3), p. 27.

the newly consecrated host within the monstrance, and the monstrance upon the altar. They would both genuflect, then the priest would offer the prayer after communion from the presider's chair.

The presider wears a white cope if the procession does not immediately follow Mass. If it does, he may change into a white cope or continue wearing the chasuble (HC 105). This draws from the late drafts,[104] updating the directions from the Roman Ritual, which required a white cope.[105] An early draft encouraged the practice: "The priest who carries the sacrament may wear the vestments of Mass in order to show better the relationship with it."[106] When a bishop presides, priests in choir dress fittingly add a cope for the procession (CB 390).

Appropriately vested, the presider blesses the incense, kneels before the altar, and incenses the Sacrament. (According to GIRM 277, he bows before and after the incensation, made with three swings, not three sets of three swings as is sometimes observed.) Receiving the humeral veil, he approaches the altar, genuflects, and takes the monstrance in hands covered by the ends of the veil. A deacon assists a presiding bishop (CB 391). These details are missing from HC 105, but presumably they apply when a priest presides. In the Roman Ritual, one of the clergy had placed a humeral veil on the shoulders of the priest, who used it to cover his hands while receiving the monstrance or repository from the deacon.[107]

Today local customs determine if ministers carry lights, incense, and a canopy (HC 105). This observation comes from the late drafts.[108] An early draft even added the option of carrying flowers.[109] This was removed, perhaps because of the

[104] Schema 403 (5), p. 28; and Schema 405 (5), p. 28.
[105] *Rituale Romanum*, Titulus X, Caput V:2, p. 803.
[106] Schema 401 (113), p. 30.
[107] *Rituale Romanum*, Titulus X, Caput V:3, pp. 803–804.
[108] Schema 403 (6), p. 28; and Schema 405 (6), p. 28.
[109] Schema 401 (113), p. 30.

seasonal nature of blooms. If some assistants carry a canopy, the priest holding the Sacrament walks beneath it.

The previous Roman Ritual had called for the same order of procession as in the major and minor litanies of St. Mark's Day and the days preceding the Ascension: the cross led the way, followed by the clergy, then the vested priest with the ministers in sacred vesture.[110] For the feast of the Purification, the Roman Ritual specified that incense led the way, and two servers with lighted candles accompanied the cross. Then the clergy followed according to their rank. The celebrant entered with the deacon on his left.[111]

The final edition of HC does not mention the order of procession, but it can be found in the Ceremonial of Bishops. A crossbearer leads the way, accompanied by servers with lighted candles. Next come "clergy," which probably means non-concelebrating priests in cassock and surplice. The deacons of the Mass come next, and then the canons and priests wearing copes, followed by concelebrants and the visiting bishops wearing copes. A minister carries the pastoral staff ahead of two others carrying burning incense. The bishop carries the Blessed Sacrament under a canopy if that is the custom. Behind him are his two assisting deacons. Other servers who carry the book and the miter come next. All may carry candles and escort the Sacrament (CB 391 and 1100).

The Ceremonial makes a provision if the bishop cannot carry the Sacrament—if, one presumes, the monstrance is heavy, the bishop is infirm, or the day is hot. In that case, the bishop walks before a priest who carries the vessel. The bishop carries the pastoral staff, and his head is bare. He does not move his hand to bless as he walks, as he would in other processions (CB 391 and 1100). The order of ministers in non-eucharistic processions is described in CB 1100 (in general), 246 (the Presentation

[110] *Rituale Romanum*, Titulus X, Caput V:2, p. 803, citing Titulus X, Caput IV:3, p. 791.

[111] *Rituale Romanum*, Titulus X, Caput II:2, p. 774.

of the Lord), 270 (Palm Sunday), 343 (the Easter Vigil), 193 (Evening Prayer), and 128 (Mass). In several of these the bishop may carry an object pertinent to the procession, such as a candle or a branch, while another minister carries the pastoral staff before him (1101). Whereas a bishop holds the pastoral staff with the curved head facing toward the people he shepherds (59), an assisting minister holding it traditionally turns it the other way.

If other bishops are present in choir dress—that is, as non-concelebrants of the Mass preceding the procession—they enter the procession behind the Blessed Sacrament. In order to keep those in higher rank nearest the Sacrament, then, concelebrating bishops in copes precede the presiding bishop in the procession, while other bishops immediately follow (CB 1100).

The Roman Ritual had described the procession of its day. The priest received the monstrance, held it against his face, turned to the people, and processed beneath a canopy accompanied by ministers, two servers carrying candles, or clergy with smoking thuribles. All walked bare-headed, carrying lighted candles and singing hymns.[112]

Local customs help determine the arrangements for a procession, guiding even the decoration of streets and squares (HC 104). A eucharistic blessing (that is, with the monstrance) may be given at stations erected along the way. The participants sing songs and offer prayers in order to keep their attention focused on Christ (HC 104, CB 392 and 1098). This paragraph is taken from the late drafts.[113]

This updates a concern from the preconciliar Roman Ritual: "The churches and walls of the streets through which one must pass are to be appropriately decorated with carpets and hangings—and with sacred images, but not profane or ostentatious

[112] *Rituale Romanum*, Titulus X, Caput V:4, p. 804.

[113] Schema 403 (4), p. 27; and Schema 405 (4), p. 27.

figures or even inappropriate decorations."[114] One can only imagine the unbecoming practices that prompted this legislation in the Middle Ages.

An early draft developed the idea:

> There may be many stations. At the stations and especially at the last one that concludes the procession, it is praiseworthy that a blessing be given. It is appropriate that a sacred reading, intercessory prayer, the Lord's Prayer, a eucharistic song, or the prayer as was indicated in the rite of benediction precede the blessing at one or another of these stations.[115]

One idea from the early draft did not carry forward: "If perhaps the sick are present at a place where the procession crosses, they may be given communion. This may take place especially before the final blessing in the church in which the path concludes."[116] In the end, communion is held completely separate from the ceremonies of exposition.

The texts for the processional hymns mentioned in HC 104 are not specified, but the ones from the fourth chapter would fittingly be used (HC 192–203), or even the responsories (204–9). Other songs could be sung in replacement of or in addition to these. The Roman Ritual had previously specified *Pange lingua* (192), *Sacris sollemniis* (193), *Verbum supernum* (194), and *Salutis humanæ Sator* (see commentary on 195), and *Æterne Rex altissime* (196). It also recommended the *Te Deum*, the *Benedictus* from Lauds, the *Magnificat* from Vespers, and, finally *Tantum ergo* (from the end of 192).[117] Any of these would still be appropriate.

[114] *Rituale Romanum*, Titulus X, Caput V:1, p. 803.
[115] Schema 401 (111), p. 30.
[116] Schema 401 (112), p. 30.
[117] *Rituale Romanum*, Titulus X, Caput V:4–5, pp. 804–811.

Ideally, the procession begins in one church and advances toward another, but for a good local reason it may return to the same church (HC 107, CB 393). This observation came from the drafts.[118]

At the end the presider imparts the blessing with the Sacrament either in the last church or in another suitable place. Then the Sacrament is reposed into the tabernacle (HC 108). This brief explanation comes from the drafts, which, however, failed even to mention the implied reposition of the Sacrament.[119]

More detail is in the Ceremonial of Bishops. When a bishop presides, all the ministers enter the sanctuary and take their places. The bishop approaches the altar, and the deacon to his right takes the monstrance from him and sets it on the altar. Those who minister genuflect. The bishop removes the humeral veil and kneels before the altar. The deacon prepares incense and presents it to the bishop for him to bless its smoke. The bishop and the deacons bow, and the bishop swings the censer three times toward the Sacrament before bowing again. The hymn *Tantum ergo* or another eucharistic hymn is sung during the incensation, which traditionally took place during the second verse and presumably follows the instructions from GIRM 277: the minister bows to the sacrament before and after swinging the censer three times. The bishop then hands the censer back to the deacon. The bishop stands and offers one of the prayers that follow the incensation in the usual form of exposition and benediction. A minister may hold the book for him. The bishop receives the humeral veil, approaches the altar, and genuflects. With the deacon assisting, he covers his hands with the ends of the humeral veil, lifts the monstrance, and makes the sign of the cross—presumably one time, not three—in silence. The deacon takes the monstrance from the bishop, sets it on the altar, and genuflects with him. While the bishop kneels, the deacon, presumably wearing the humeral

[118] Schema 403 (7), p. 28; and Schema 405 (7), p. 28.

[119] Schema 403 (8), p. 28; and Schema 405 (8), p. 28.

veil, takes the Sacrament from the monstrance to the place of reservation. The people may sing an acclamation, and the procession returns to the sacristy in the usual way (CB 394).

Although this outline pertains to a presiding bishop, many of the steps would be followed by a presiding priest. He conducts the blessing and reposition as indicated for the more usual forms of Benediction not preceded by a procession.

Eucharistic Congresses

As *Eucharisticum Mysterium* treated eucharistic congresses in its final paragraphs, so does HC. A congress of this sort includes presentations giving greater understanding of the Eucharist, devotions, private prayers, processions, and, most importantly, the Mass. When celebrated for a region, several churches may offer perpetual adoration (EM 67).

One host community or "station" invites the local Church, regional churches, or the global Church to come understand some aspect of the mystery and to worship publicly in a bond of love and unity. Congresses are to be a true sign of faith and love by means of this participation (HC 109).

The first eucharistic congresses took place in the late nineteenth century at Lille, France. Other localities immediately copied the idea, and such gatherings have remained popular ever since.[120] The first international eucharistic congress was organized at the university in Lille by Marie Marthe Emilia Tamisier, a student of St. Peter Julian Eymard, the French priest who promoted eucharistic devotion and founded the Congregation of the Blessed Sacrament. Having secured the support of Pope Leo XIII, Tamisier succeeded in gathering many people to celebrate their devotion.[121]

[120] Martimort II, p. 252.

[121] Lane, pp. 10–11. Martimort gives 1873 as the date; Lane gives 1881, assigning the earlier date to a local conference at Paray-le-Monial, where Margaret Mary Alacoque promoted devotion to the Sacred Heart.

An early draft explained how congresses were to be based on Scripture, tradition, and the Second Vatican Council. Although the subsequent drafts rewrote this section into the paragraphs that remain, the early draft reveals the perspective developing a few years after EM had introduced its treatment of congresses in 1967:

> 115. The communion of charity that is accomplished by participation in the one bread and of the same cup (1 Cor 10:16-17), not only gathers members of each local Church to themselves, but also brings it about that Christian communities dispersed around the entire globe may unite into one, holy, catholic Church.
>
> For, although a local Church may be built up by all means of salvation, and it may plainly manifest especially through the celebration of the Eucharist "the symbol . . . of that charity and 'unity of the mystical body, without which there can be no salvation' " (*Lumen Gentium* 26; S. Th. III, 73, 3), nevertheless to a great extent the action of the Holy Spirit precedes that of the congregation so that it may intend to show the universal communion of the churches as a sign of the entire human race gathered together (LG 1).
>
> 116. For this reason, from the beginnings of the Church, this unity was promoted by the Eucharist aptly signified and marvelously realized (LG 11) in various initiatives.
>
> In these most recent times a new manner has been expressed, in which the faithful, desiring to offer honor to the Lord in the enduring Sacrament, declaring public praises and prayers, began to meet to celebrate Eucharistic Congresses.
>
> Indeed, the renewal of this initiative must be in accord with the mind of the Second Vatican Council—from which certain principles are proposed for places where this pious custom is in force and seems to be able to be adapted to the conditions of the present time.
>
> 117. Therefore, a local church inviting churches from the same nation or the entire world to celebrate a eucharistic congress with it must strictly show above all the connected tables of the Divine Word and the Body of Christ (SC 47; S. Augustine, *Trac-*

> *tate on John* 6:13, PL 35:1613), and it must similarly take care by its manner of living to bring to reality the communion of charity expressed by the sacred meal.
>
> Since the Eucharist is "the source and the summit of all preaching of the Gospel" (*Presbyterorum ordinis* 5), it will help so to prepare and arrange the form of these celebrations that it takes a powerful aim—whether it expresses the life of the people of God coming to maturity in the young churches, in which "the community of faith, liturgy and charity" (*Ad Gentes* 19) grows in harmony together, or the fuller transformation of human society in older churches of age, the pledge of which is manifest in the sacrament (*Gaudium et spes* 38).[122]

In preparation for congresses, the local church and other churches should study the place, theme, and program. These consider the needs of the people and foster theological study and the good of the local church, utilizing the assistance of experts in various fields (HC 110). These recommendations originated in the late drafts.[123]

Congresses are to follow a threefold purpose: catechesis suited to the abilities of different groups; more active participation in the liturgy, especially in hearing the Word of God and forming a community; and the implementation of social works for human development (HC 111).

The second of these goals, hearing the Word and forming a community, cites the Constitutions on the Sacred Liturgy (41–52) and on the Church (26). It shows that congresses ultimately lead not just to better private worship of the sacramental presence of Christ, but to better communal participation in the liturgy. This goal also fosters devotion to Christ present in his Word, not only in the sacrament of his Body.

The last of these goals, implementing social works, explores a range of possibilities, such as sharing temporal goods as the

[122] Schema 401 (115–17), pp. 30–31.

[123] Schema 403 (2), p. 28; and Schema 405 (2), p. 28.

first Christians did (Acts 4:32) in order to spread the gospel from the eucharistic table. This goal calls the gospel a force of growth in the world today and the pledge of future glory, a reference to *Unitatis redintegratio*, the council's Decree on Church Unity (15).

These three recommended goals appeared in an early draft and were copied over through the others into the final version. HC 111 reclaims that complete thread. The drafts also cited SC 47 in addition to *Unitatis redintegratio* 15 as the source for the third goal. There the Constitution on the Sacred Liturgy, citing St. Augustine's *Tractate on John* 6:13, frames the gift of the Eucharist at the Last Supper as a sacrament of love, a sign of unity, and a bond of charity.[124] The Eucharist demands more than interior devotion.

The section concludes with several criteria for a congress (HC 112). As with the previous number, all of these points appeared in the drafts from the earliest stage.[125]

The celebration of the congress Mass should be the source and summit toward which forms of piety are directed (HC 112a). This makes an uncited allusion to the council's Dogmatic Constitution on the Church (*Lumen Gentium* 11). Both the later drafts erroneously cited EM 57 instead of EM 67 as the source. The final version of HC corrected it.

Celebrations of the Word of God, catechetical sessions, and public speeches should explore the congress theme and carry out its practical aspects (HC 112b). These points were all introduced earlier (HC 110 and 111). This summary demonstrates the integration of the aspects of a congress around a theme to enhance its effectiveness.

Participants are to have access to the exposed Blessed Sacrament for common prayers or extended adoration in different churches suited for the devotion (HC 112c). This presumes that

[124] Schema 401 (118), p. 32; Schema 403 (3), p. 29; and Schema 405 (3), p. 29.
[125] Schema 401 (119), p. 32; Schema 403 (4), p. 29; and Schema 405 (4), p. 29.

a regional congress shares multiple locations where the faithful may conveniently find opportunities for prayer. All the drafts cited EM 67 for this point, which clarifies its regional vision.

Any eucharistic procession taking place at the congress is to follow the appropriate norms (HC 101–8), accounting for local social and religious conditions while providing common hymns and prayers. The reminder at 112d collates the criteria for a congress in one place.

These paragraphs mark a first attempt at universal regulations for a practice that developed at the grassroots. Originating only in the late nineteenth century, such congresses became possible due to increased eucharistic devotion, the improvement of mass communication, and the developing means of affordable long-distance travel. Eucharistic congresses use modern circumstances to revive ancient belief.

Eucharistic Reservations

Outside Mass, the real presence of Jesus Christ endures. His sacramental presence under the form of bread stored in tabernacles serves for Viaticum, communion outside Mass, and the adoration of the faithful. All of these purposes supply opportunities for spiritual enrichment through eucharistic reservation. Yet, they also call attention to some eucharistic reservations.

Viaticum

The renewal of rites for the sick and the dying has been one of the greatest successes and one of the greatest failures of the postconciliar liturgical reform. On the positive side, Catholics have largely received the message that the sacrament of anointing is no longer reserved for the dying. Known to the preconciliar Church as "extreme unction," its administration had signaled that death was near. Now those in advanced age, those anticipating surgery, and those with a serious illness are all candidates for anointing. This has led to a wider celebration of the sacrament, which only a priest may administer, and to a common usage of the reformed expression "anointing of the sick" to show its purpose.

A priest may still visit and anoint a dying person, but the preferred time for anointing is during the illness when the properties of oil align with prayers for healing. Once death is near, other prayers are more appropriate for the dying, especially if they have already been anointed during their illness.

The Church offers an array of prayers that some minister may lead for the sick: when making a simple visit, hearing a confession, bringing communion, anointing, accompanying the dying, and interceding after death has occurred. A priest is required only for the sacraments of confession and anointing. A deacon or an instituted or deputed minister may bring Holy Communion and Viaticum. Anyone may visit, and anyone may offer the appropriate prayers for the dying and for the dead. All of these services are among the official rites of the Church.

Yet in the minds of many, Catholics and non-Catholics alike, the Church has a single thing called "last rites" that requires the presence of a priest. An instituted extraordinary lay minister of Holy Communion is capable of bringing Viaticum, and any lay person may offer the Church's other prayers for the dying and prayers for the dead, all of which are by definition last rites that do not require a priest.

Of all these, the sacrament for which the Church has the greatest concern is communion under the form of Viaticum (canon 921 §1). To receive it, a Catholic is to be near death but still able to communicate and to swallow.

However, caregivers for dying Catholics frequently seem unaware of this. They have not learned the importance of requesting Viaticum while the person is still conscious. Many of them wait until the person has slipped into unconsciousness to request "last rites" from a priest when, sadly, it is too late to offer what would help the most: Viaticum.

The first purpose of eucharistic reservation is to provide this sacrament to the dying. Yet many churches arrange the sacred furnishings in a way implying that the first purpose of the tabernacle is for the adoration of the people and the convenience of their communion—even during Mass.

Catholics and non-Catholics alike would surely benefit from more catechesis on the significance of Viaticum in the life of the Church. Attention may also be given to the placement and decoration of tabernacles, so that the Church's care for the dying is more evident.

Holy Communion outside Mass

Parishes sometimes offer communion services when daily Mass is not possible, usually due to the unavailability of a priest. The group that gathers for daily Mass, devoted to the Eucharist, may receive communion outside Mass instead. This fulfills their desire for receiving communion, even though it does not fully engage their full, conscious, active participation in the offering of sacrifice. They may hear the lectionary readings of the day, recite prayers in common, and enter a ritual with other believers—all of which fulfill some of their daily spiritual yearnings.

The same may happen on a Sunday, especially in areas where priests are few and remote. The deacon or lay minister who leads the service frequently includes the distribution of communion, largely because of the devotion and expectations of the people.

Yet the Church offers other forms of communal prayer, notably Morning and Evening Prayer from the Liturgy of the Hours. These too are intended for the use of the faithful. On a weekday without Mass, the faithful would appropriately pray one of these offices in common. However, in practice, they may be unfamiliar with this form of daily prayer, making it awkward in a communal setting and unsatisfying in its observance. Many would likely gather, pray, look at the tabernacle, and wonder why they did not receive communion after making the effort to come to church.

Catholic piety has a strong foundation in communion, even when the celebration of the Eucharist is not possible. This shows the centrality of this sacrament in the lives of Catholics, but it also shows how readily Catholics want to receive communion even if they are not participating in the sacrifice of the Mass. They seek the reward of the sacrament without the full personal investment in the sacrifice.

The expectation for communion services questions how Catholics perceive their participation at Mass. Some arrive late, receive communion, and leave early, clearly seeking the sacrament without fully participating in the Mass. That mindset, fed by centuries of an Order of Mass that did not include the communion of the faithful, expects communion to be available when Mass is not.

For some, the shorter form of communion outside Mass is preferable to communion within Mass. Anxious to get on with their day, they receive communion and leave church after only a few minutes of prayer.

Others, though, express indignation when Mass is not available. At a time and place in history when priests are few, parishes are closing, and Mass schedules have been reduced, Catholics rightly wonder where the priests are.

In the United States, the decrease in vocations to the priesthood has prompted an increase of extern priests who charitably sacrifice their homeland, family, and friends to serve as missionaries to a country that used to provide missionaries for the world. Some of these priests endure the prejudice that some Americans harbor against foreigners, even as they face the anti-immigration sentiment that pervades many municipalities both urban and rural. Consumer-minded Catholics accustomed to ordering goods online have settled for the commodified solution: if it is hard to generate priestly vocations at home, import them from abroad. Love for the Mass is driving this trend: Catholics need priests, no matter where they are from.

Receiving communion outside Mass is never ideal. It is a benefit designed especially for the sick who are unable to come to church. Unfortunately, it has become a benefit offered to healthy Catholics who have no available priest.

Eucharistic Adoration

Many Catholics add eucharistic adoration to the plan of their spiritual life. Placing themselves in the sacramental presence of Christ, they spend up to an hour in regular devotional prayer. For many, the practice puts into context the lesser concerns of their day and centers their lives on Christ. Many understandably prefer to conduct their prayer when the Blessed Sacrament is exposed. Yet even without exposition, Christ is fully present in the consecrated hosts of a ciborium secured inside a closed tabernacle.

The opening sentence of HC cautions that for the whole Church the center of the Christian life is the celebration of the Eucharist, the Mass. Adoration has its place in the Christian life, but never alone; it is always in balance with the celebration of the Eucharist (HC 4). The theme repeats in the introductory material to the forms of eucharistic adoration (80, 82). Believers best interact with the sacrament of the Body and Blood of Christ when they receive communion at Mass.

Some Catholic adults attend Mass but do not receive communion, a phenomenon especially noteworthy within the Latino community. Some remain in irregular second marriages due to a divorce for which they have never opened an investigation of nullity. Others remain in unmarried relationships unimpeded by any canon law, due to the inaccessible costs of the wedding celebration that they deem socially acceptable. Others refrain from receiving communion not because of a marital situation but because they simply feel unworthy of the sacrament. Some of these Catholics abide in a complacent culture that reveres the Eucharist without feeling impelled to receive it.

This pious reticence was more widespread throughout the Catholic world in the nineteenth century when eucharistic congresses developed. Weekly communion was rare. Some parish organizations met at church once a month for a Mass in order to encourage members to receive communion that frequently. Individuals would go to confession the day before in order to prepare, as many Catholics learned that confession was required before every communion. If frequent confession seemed burdensome, Catholics abstained from communion.

The Mass served instead as a grand experience of eucharistic adoration, especially during the consecration.

Since the thirteenth century, communion had become obligatory for Catholics at least once a year; many were not even going that frequently. In 1905 Pope St. Pius X issued and approved his Congregation for Divine Worship's Decree on Frequent and Daily Reception of Holy Communion, *Sacra Tridentina*.[1] That restored more frequent communion around the world, but it made little impact in Latin America. Perhaps still reechoing the catechesis of missionaries, Catholics there seem to have never fully embraced the importance of receiving communion during every Mass.

Adoration is not a substitute for receiving Holy Communion. Those in a situation that in their judgment bars them from sharing at the eucharistic table best accomplish all that they can to correct the circumstances so that they may receive again. A healthy eucharistic spirituality begins with communion at Mass and includes auxiliary periods of eucharistic adoration.

During periods of exposition, many people enjoy silence. However, HC promotes communal activities: readings from Scripture, a homily or exhortation, and singing, in addition to silent prayer (HC 95–96). In reality, many people's lives are filled with so much sound and background noise that they appreciate disengaging from it. Visually, those who spend a large part of their day before a video screen seek time away to look at nothing in particular except the religious imagery of the exposed Sacrament.

Even so, communal prayer before the Blessed Sacrament is to include communal spiritual exercises. At the end of the Holy

[1] Pope Pius X, *Sacra Tridentina: Motu Proprio De Examinibus Ordinandorum in Urbe* (July 16, 1905), https://www.vatican.va/content/pius-x/la/motu_proprio/documents/hf_p-x_motu-proprio_19050716_sacrosancta-tridentina-synodus.html.

Thursday Mass of the Lord's Supper, the faithful spend time at prayer before the Blessed Sacrament in the tabernacle. The Vatican's Circular Letter on the Preparation and Celebration of the Easter Feasts recommends on that occasion the proclamation of excerpts from Jesus's final discourse at the Last Supper (John 13–17).[2] The same model of periodic public readings applies to any celebration of exposition.

Some activities decidedly would not be appropriate. Doing homework, texting friends, catching up on email, or using one's cellular device for other secular activities belong outside the period of exposition. The purpose of this time is devoting oneself to Christ, not to distractions (HC 95). Exposition is not visual background music for the performance of other tasks.

Some communities offer the sacrament of reconciliation during periods of exposition. Neither HC nor the Order of Penance envisions the practice. The Vatican reluctantly permits the hearing of confessions during the celebration of Mass in order to meet the needs of the faithful (*Redemptionis Sacramentum* 76).[3] However, the sacrament of reconciliation may not be united to Mass in such a way that it becomes a single celebration. These are distinct sacraments and independent liturgies.

The priest celebrating Mass may not interrupt it to hear confessions. The same would logically apply to the people. Those in attendance are expected to participate fully, consciously, and actively in the entire liturgical event, be it Mass or reconciliation. A person would not be fulfilling their respon-

[2] Congregation for Divine Worship, "Circular Letter on the Preparation and Celebration of Easter Feasts," February 20, 1988, no. 56, https://www.ewtn.com/catholicism/library/circular-letter-concerning-preparation-and-celebration-of-easter-feasts-2168.

[3] Congregation for Divine Worship and the Discipline of the Sacraments, Instruction *Redemptionis Sacramentum*, (On certain matters to be observed or to be avoided regarding the Most Holy Eucharist), March 25, 2004, https://www.vatican.va/roman_curia/congregations/ccdds/documents/rc_con_ccdds_doc_20040423_redemptionis-sacramentum_en.html.

sibility to participate at Mass if they withdraw from it for a separate celebration of sacramental confession, even if only for a few minutes. Similarly, those spending time in eucharistic adoration are not to participate at Mass in a nearby space (HC 83).

By application, then, those participating in the liturgy of exposition and benediction, in order to devote themselves to Christ, ideally do not engage in a separate liturgy such as reconciliation at the same time. The Order of Penance permits the celebration of reconciliation at any time and on any day, but it encourages penitents to find a time apart from Mass (13). Logically, the same separation would apply to another celebration, such as baptism outside Mass, confirmation outside Mass, communion outside Mass, and eucharistic adoration.

Some priests offer adoration before Mass begins, apparently to help the faithful focus on the sacrament that they are about to receive. The ritual book never encourages this. In fact, it envisions that exposition comes afterward, using a host consecrated at that Mass to continue one's appreciation of the communion just received (HC 94). HC does not forbid exposition before Mass, probably because it never envisioned that someone would do it. Neither in the preconciliar liturgy nor the postconciliar drafts does the practice appear. Those who come to Mass early may easily worship the Blessed Sacrament in the tabernacle.

If exposition takes place, it involves its own liturgy with ministers, vestments, candles, incense, and music. There is no provision for setting the Sacrament out for adoration and then putting it back without these liturgical parts and in that liturgical context. Worship without such elements may take place at any time before a tabernacle. Exposition of the Blessed Sacrament implies much more. The primary point of gathering the faithful for Mass is the authentic celebration of Mass, which does not include a prelude of adoration before the exposed Sacrament.

Some churches offensively and illicitly provide automated devices encouraging the faithful to create and conclude periods of exposition at will. For example, an individual may enter the church, push a button, and reveal a monstrance-bearing host, either by parting a curtain or raising the vessel into position from a concealed area. The liturgical books make no provision for such a do-it-yourself approach. Exposition of the Blessed Sacrament requires a priest or a deacon, and, if neither is available, then an instituted acolyte or deputed extraordinary minister of Holy Communion. Individuals may not otherwise expose or repose the Sacrament. In the absence of a liturgy, people may pray before a tabernacle.

During extended adoration, if the faithful cannot sustain the practice throughout a lengthy period, an appropriate minister is to repose the Sacrament at previously announced times (HC 88). Reportedly, in some parishes, some of the faithful have been told instead to cover the monstrance with a cloth, leaving the vessel on the altar. The Blessed Sacrament demands more careful attention. The liturgy gives instructions for the proper reposition of the Sacrament, and it requires an appropriate minister.

Some questionable devotional practices have evolved. Near the start of the COVID-19 pandemic, some priests took a monstrance into the skies in a private plane or helicopter, inviting airborne adoration and blessing of the people. Others held the monstrance in the back end of a pickup truck. However, HC 101 expects all processions to be conducted with dignity and reverence.

In place of a eucharistic procession from one sacred space to another, some ministers incorrectly process the monstrance through the assembly gathered in a single place, moving it like a celebrity amid fawning fans. In some cases, the minister invites individuals to touch the monstrance or presents it to the faces of individual believers in turn. HC makes no provision for these practices. The Blessed Sacrament is the Body of Christ and deserves the adoration of the faithful. It is not a lamp, a rock star, or a curio. The devotion of the faithful is admirable, but HC establishes certain expectations on how this devotion is exercised. The ultimate encounter is not outside Mass when the Sacrament is processed and presented to the faithful, but during Mass when the faithful process and present themselves to receive the sacrament in Holy Communion.

The Celebration of the Eucharist

Some practices of eucharistic devotion are entering the celebration of the Mass where they are ill suited because the missal does not envision them. When it comes to the Body and Blood of Christ, the rubrics are most concerned about the communion of the faithful. They make room for appropriate moments of adoration; however, the primary aim of Mass is not to practice personal adoration, but to fulfill the requests of Jesus to eat his Body, drink his Blood, and to do this in memory of him.

The Tabernacle

Tabernacles are no longer to be located on the altar, as they once were. This helps avoid confusing the faithful about the purpose of the celebration of the Eucharist, which features the consecration and communion of the Body and Blood of Christ upon the altar (EM 55), not the adoration and distribution of previously consecrated hosts from the tabernacle. In the sanctuary of a Catholic church, the center of the congregation's attention is to be the altar, not the tabernacle (GIRM 299). The objects specifically mentioned to be on or near the altar are the cross and candles (GIRM 117).

In many churches the tabernacle takes its place along the center axis together with the cross and the altar. During incensation, the cross and the altar are reverenced together both near the opening of Mass and during the preparation of the gifts (GIRM 49, 277). However, if the tabernacle sits beneath the cross, the visual impact may signal to the faithful that the priest is incensing the tabernacle and the altar instead of the cross and the altar. The cross with the image of Christ crucified provides a visual cue to the purpose of the altar where the sacramental representation of the mystery of the cross takes place (GIRM 122, 308).

Tabernacles ideally occupy places suitable to the private prayer of the people (HC 9). Especially at places with many visitors, the tabernacle is preferably located in a separate chapel away from the main body of the church. Other churches would laudably follow a similar practice to make clear the distinction between the celebration of Mass and the purpose of tabernacles. The missal prefers that the presidential chair occupy the area at the back of the sanctuary, though it admits that sometimes the tabernacle is there (GIRM 310).

The third edition of the missal added some unexpected specifications in its General Instruction in the year 2000. Accepting that tabernacles were not to be placed on the main altar, it assigned judgment on the location of tabernacles to the diocesan bishop. It offered two options in this order: placement in the sanctuary, even on an old altar there, or in a separate chapel organically connected to the church and visible to the faithful (GIRM 315).

This new paragraph revised the one from the previous edition of the GIRM, which took a position more in keeping with EM and HC:

> Every encouragement should be given to the practice of eucharistic reservation in a chapel suited to the faithful's private adoration and prayer. If this is impossible because of the structure of the church, the sacrament should be reserved at an altar or elsewhere, in keeping with local custom, and in a part of the church that is worthy and properly adorned (276).[4]

[4] Congregation for Divine Worship and the Discipline of the Sacraments, General Instruction of the Roman Missal, https://www.catholicculture.org/culture/library/view.cfm?recnum=5139.

The revision perhaps reflects fears of the lost importance of eucharistic reservation and implies that tabernacles play a more central role in the Mass than the rest of the missal promotes. However, reservation derives from Mass, not Mass from reservation.

In some parishes candles are set next to the tabernacle and lighted during Mass, even though the GIRM never calls for that. It limits the usage of candles in relationship to the altar (117, 307) and in processions (120, 274). Lighted candles at the tabernacle invite the faithful to focus on an object that does not directly pertain to the celebration of the Mass, as does the altar.

Although the common celebration of Mass in a parish includes the distribution of communion to the faithful from the tabernacle, the liturgical documents repeatedly make a case against it. The Second Vatican Council said, "The more perfect form of participation in the Mass whereby the faithful, after the priest's communion, receive the Lord's body from the same sacrifice, is warmly recommended" (SC 55).[5] The missal declares, "It is most desirable that the faithful, just as the Priest himself is bound to do, receive the Lord's Body from hosts consecrated at the same Mass" (GIRM 85). Both these citations also recommend communion under both kinds, stressing participation in the communion effected in the same celebration. Similarly, the introduction of HC states, "Sacramental Communion received within Mass is the more perfect participation in the Eucharistic Celebration. The Eucharistic sign is expressed more clearly, when the faithful receive the Body of the Lord after the Communion of the Priest, from the same Sacrifice" (13).

When the faithful regularly receive communion from the tabernacle, unlike the priest who always receives his communion from the altar, the practice magnifies the importance

[5] *Vatican Council II*, pp. 136–37.

of the tabernacle for the faithful and separates their participation in the Mass from that of the priest. Many of the faithful see the tabernacle as the source of their communion, and, unsurprisingly then, the most important furnishing for a parish church. This perception impairs their sense of being the priestly people completing the sacrifice that they are making at the altar at each Eucharist. Instead, they receive the fruit of someone else's sacrifice. They are effectively participating in a communion service outside Mass inside Mass, as the preconciliar rubrics required.

The proper use of gestures during the Mass further focuses the attention of the faithful on the altar. "If, however, the tabernacle with the Most Blessed Sacrament is situated in the sanctuary, the Priest, the Deacon, and the other ministers genuflect when they approach the altar [at the beginning of Mass] and when they depart from it [at the end of Mass], but not during the celebration of Mass itself" (GIRM 274). When ministers pass from one side of the sanctuary to the other between the altar and the tabernacle *during* the celebration of Mass, they are to make a deep bow to the *altar*, not a genuflection to the tabernacle (CB 72). These gestures support reverences to the tabernacle outside Mass, but during Mass the tabernacle cedes importance to the altar of sacrifice. This helps explain why the postconciliar Church moved tabernacles off the top of altars.

The missal never describes the common practice of bringing previously consecrated hosts from the tabernacle to the altar at communion time of the Mass. It offers no advice on reverences at that moment because it prefers that ministers not distribute previously consecrated hosts to those who are actively participating at Mass. When ministers do approach the tabernacle during Mass, they judge for themselves what reverence is best.

Because the newly consecrated bread and wine is sitting on the altar, a genuflection made to the tabernacle may suggest that the previously consecrated hosts there are more sacred than the newly consecrated ones on the altar. Outside Mass, when the minister brings the ciborium from the tabernacle to the altar, he or she genuflects not when approaching the tabernacle, but only after the hosts have been placed on the altar (HC 30). This seems to justify avoiding a genuflection upon opening the tabernacle during the communion rite of the Mass.

Some ministers execute a genuflection upon returning the hosts to the tabernacle. Nonetheless, GIRM 274 could be interpreted to mean that the genuflection toward the tabernacle at the end of Mass covers the reverence at reposition after communion.

The imprecise observance of such rubrics has led some the faithful to perform well-intentioned but questionable devotions during Mass:

- In churches where the tabernacle occupies a space in a side chapel, some of the faithful choose a devotional place for Mass in close proximity to it, rather than to the altar where they are to participate as the priestly people.
- A communion minister receives a ciborium of newly consecrated hosts from the priest and then turns toward the tabernacle to bow before moving to a station to distribute communion, as if the tabernacle is holier than the Body of Christ in the vessel in hand.
- A communicant upon receiving the Body of Christ turns toward the tabernacle and genuflects before returning to the pew, again suggesting that the Body of Christ is in the tabernacle, not in their mouth.
- A communicant upon receiving the sacrament goes to the Blessed Sacrament chapel to kneel in the sacramental presence of Christ, as if what they received was something inferior.

All these actions, unsupported by any documentation yet springing from a misguided sense of respect, demonstrate that the Church has poorly catechized people on the meaning of eucharistic communion. This surely results from the unabated practice of distributing communion to the faithful from the tabernacle at virtually every Mass.

The Consecration

In the past, especially during the Middle Ages, when Catholics rarely received communion at Mass, the consecration provided the highlight when they could behold and adore the sacramental presence of Christ in the host and chalice. The consecration is important, but it leads directly toward communion.

After citing the words of Christ, the priest shows the host to the people (OM 89, for example). Both the preconciliar and postconciliar rubrics describe his action the same way, with the Latin word *ostendit*. However, prior to the council, with his back to the people, the only way for the priest to show the host was to raise it above his head. This made it look like an elevation, a word that has entered the English translation of the GIRM multiple times, even where the Latin word indicates a showing instead.[6] At the consecration, while facing the people, the priest more appropriately shows the host and chalice by bringing them forward rather than up. He is not elevating the elements to the Father; he is showing them to the people, who appropriately adore.

The priest genuflects in adoration (OM 89, for example). Prior to the conciliar reforms, he also genuflected before showing the host to the people. The elimination of the first genuflection invites a more deliberate focus on the genuflection in adoration that remains. Some priests take extended time for this action, which threatens to interrupt the sweeping content of the entire eucharistic prayer. The descriptive rubric is the same as the preconciliar one, the only difference being the

[6] Paul Turner, *Ars Celebrandi: Celebrating and Concelebrating Mass* (Collegeville, MN: Liturgical Press, 2021), pp. 106–9.

number of times it appears. The missal seems intent on preserving the flow of eucharistic prayer, all of which is important, and not to let it come to a stop as if the consecration pauses or ends the prayer.

A server may ring a small bell if appropriate (GIRM 150). The permission does not appear within the Order of Mass itself, which details the essential words and actions of the celebration. In the preconciliar rubrics, the minister rang the bell three times at each elevation, but the postconciliar missal removed the number "three," thus implying a single ring instead. The diminished number of rings complements the diminished number of genuflections. Still, in many churches the server performs the preconciliar instruction as if to draw more attention to the showing of the elements than the missal envisions.

Incense may be used at the consecration (GIRM 276). In some locations, servers with candles take up positions on either side of the one preparing to incense the Blessed Sacrament. The Vatican made provision for this in large scale celebrations, such as those outdoors in St. Peter's Square, to enhance the adoration of the faithful by helping them see where the showing of the host and chalice was taking place.[7] In normal circumstances the rubrics permit only incense, not candles. The Mass pauses for a moment of adoration. It keeps the focus on the entire eucharistic prayer with its moments of praise and petition.

Fragments

The breaking of bread produces crumbs. Throughout the Mass, the rubrics treat these fragments with care. This is not

[7] Congregatio de Culto Divino et Disciplina Sacramentorum, *Guida per le Grandi Celebrazioni*, June 13, 2014, par. 27, https://www.vatican.va/roman_curia/congregations/ccdds/documents/rc_con_ccdds_doc_20140613_guida-grandi-celebrazioni_it.html.

just any bread, but the Body of Christ, so the crumbs receive attention.

For example, "Whenever a fragment of the host adheres to his fingers, especially after the fraction or after the Communion of the faithful, the Priest should wipe his fingers over the paten or, if necessary, wash them. Likewise, he should also gather any fragments that may have fallen outside the paten" (GIRM 278). The missal does not consider fragments an everyday concern. There may be instances when the priest needs to deal with them, but the instruction is not punctilious. If the priest notices fragments on his fingers, he may simply brush them together to dislodge the fragments over the paten. Washing fingers with water is a last resort, not a daily instruction.

After communion the priest or the deacon is to return to the altar to collect any fragments that may remain (GIRM 163, 183). Again, the rubrics suggest he may not find any, but they exercise caution without obsession.

Should a host fall, the minister is to pick it up "reverently" (GIRM 280), but the rubric says nothing more. What is the minister to do next? In many cases the minister or communicant may consume the host, but it could also be fittingly brought to the sacristy for dilution in water to be poured down the sacrarium. The rubric makes no mention of fragments, nor does it say that the area where a host has fallen needs to be washed with water.

In the past, after the consecration, the priest was expected to press together his "canonical digits," the thumb and forefinger that had touched the host, in order to limit the falling of fragments. This instruction has been removed from the missal, another indication that concern for fragments is not to be exaggerated.

For the manufacturing of bread, the missal prefers that it have the appearance of food so that it can be broken into parts to be shared by some of the faithful (GIRM 321). Even so, parishes commonly use small hosts, effectively pre-broken bread, a convenience that avoids causing many fragments. The missal shows less concern over reducing the number of fragments of the sacramental Body of Christ than in distributing broken bread as a sign of the unity of those receiving and becoming the Body of Christ in communion.

A review of these rubrics may surprise some Catholics, but the missal is not excessively worried about fragments. It treats them with respect, but it keeps its focus on the full, conscious, active participation in the Eucharist, which reaches its climax not in an exaggerated reverence for fragments, but in sacramental communion.

Receiving Communion

The catechism stresses that in communion the faithful receive the body, blood, soul, and divinity of Jesus Christ (1374). This formula, popularized in the divine mercy chaplet, appears also in the missal (GIRM 9), which cites the Council of Trent as its source. Some Catholics adopt this teaching to justify the practice of receiving communion only under the form of bread, because, according to the Church's teaching of concomitance, the bread is not only the Body of Christ, but also his blood. Yet the missal cites this very teaching in order to promote communion under both kinds, which "reflects more fully the sacred realities that the Liturgy signifies."[8]

Furthermore, the missal offers catechesis on receiving the Blood of Christ where this is permitted, a practice it calls "a fuller form." It signifies the eucharistic banquet more clearly. It shows how the new and eternal covenant was ratified in the blood of the Lord, and it connects the Mass to the eschatological banquet (GIRM 281). Yes, to receive communion under one form is to receive the entire Christ, but receiving under both forms is a fuller sign.

[8] *Norms for the Distribution and Reception of Holy Communion*, par. 11.

By receiving only the sacred host, communicants put themselves at risk of not receiving from the sacrifice actually being celebrated because of the widespread practice of offering communion under one form, distributed to the faithful from the tabernacle. The missal is anxious that the proper use of signs display the active participation of the people.

The music at communion sometimes overlooks the distinction between the sacrifice of the Mass and eucharistic reservation. Some hymns chosen for communion focus on belief in the real presence of Christ. The music that HC 192–99 recommends for eucharistic adoration is not designed to be sung at Mass, yet in some gatherings it is. The liturgy has provided a moment of adoration during the consecration. During communion the focus has shifted.

The missal provides an ample array of antiphons to inspire the choice of music at communion. Surprising to many, these rarely make self-references to the communion underway. Many of them, in fact, cite the gospel from the same Mass. They connect the presence of Christ in the table of the Word and his presence at the table of the Eucharist, a connection that HC 111 favors as well. As the gospel forms the basis for living a life of faithful discipleship, so communion nourishes the Christian to reenter the world with the grace of the sacrament. Communion music that focuses on adoring the Blessed Sacrament removes these nuances.

The posture of the faithful when receiving communion varies according to the preferences of the conferences of bishops. In the United States, the posture is standing, unless an individual chooses to kneel (GIRM 160). Although the bishops do not explain their decision, it proves wise given the other postures that the faithful assume during Mass and the long tradition of the Church.

The priest is always standing when he addresses prayer to the Father. The people do as well, with the sole exception of their kneeling throughout most of the eucharistic prayer. In the United States, they stand with the priest for the preface, but then kneel for a longer period than the universal General Instruction envisions. When prayers address God, the liturgy prefers that people stand. Furthermore, all stand for the proclamation of the gospel and for declaring the creed. St. Basil the Great wrote that standing to pray reminds the faithful of the resurrection; they have been raised with Christ and seek the things that are above. Basil held that standing also shows that the Lord's day presents an image of the age to come (*The Holy Spirit* 27). Some Catholics like to kneel at communion out of respect for the real presence of Christ, but standing at communion demonstrates faith in the resurrection of Christ, who comes in the form of this sacrament.

As a sign of reverence, the USCCB recommends not kneeling for communion but a bow of the head before receiving the sacrament while standing (GIRM 160). If this were performed uniformly, it would demonstrate the unity of the Body of Christ in faith and practice. Virtually every Catholic is capable of bowing the head; not all are capable of kneeling.

Still, the faithful exercise a variety of gestures at this point. Some bow the head as requested, but others bow from the waist. Some genuflect, a gesture made by the priest before his communion, and one that not even the deacon makes before receiving his. Some communicants sign themselves with the cross. Some do a combination of these actions. Some do nothing. This opportunity for uniform expression of reverence for the Eucharist has diversified into a pattern so prevalent in American society, doing things one's own way.

The communicant may receive in the mouth or in the hand, and the choice belongs to the communicant (GIRM 160, 161). In either case, the faithful approach like beggars, receiving, not taking. Yet sometimes at the first communion of children, those responsible for the liturgy require the children to receive on the mouth and while kneeling out of a false belief that this is more reverent toward the real presence of Christ. Even children have the right to choose how to receive communion—in the mouth or in the hand. And they should learn from the beginning what posture the USCCB prefers, demonstrating even by standing the unity of the Body of Christ.

In the past children commonly learned not to chew the host, but to let it dissolve on their tongue. Some educators mistakenly thought it was irreverent to chew the Body of Christ, as if it would maim the Son of God. The faithful eat the sacramental presence of the risen Jesus, not the physical presence of the earthly Jesus. Besides, his command was indeed to eat his flesh. This is spiritual food unlike any other, but it is still food. Again, the emphasis is on communion.

The vocabulary for the vessels sets their function apart. Instead of "cup" and "bowl," the missal refers to "chalice" and "paten" (GIRM 327). These terms help identify the sacredness of the gathering, but they are not intended to remove the experience from its purpose as a meal.

Some of the faithful not planning to receive communion join the procession and place themselves before the priest or the minister seeking a blessing. A grassroots practice has evolved in which they cross their hands on their chest, indicating that they are not receiving communion. The Church has no official position on this; the custom has spread on its own.

Yet communion is not a time for blessings; it is a time for communion. The practice shows another disconnection between the offering of sacrifice and the reception of communion. Especially in parishes where communion is distributed regularly from the tabernacle at Mass, the people do not experience the integrity of communion within the sacrifice. They may then see no problem approaching the minister for some other purpose. After all, those who approach for the purpose of receiving communion from the same sacrifice are often receiving communion from a different source.

An appropriate action for those who will not receive is to wait at their place until communion is over and receive the blessing at the end of Mass. Of course, the best solution is to resolve the issue keeping them from communion so that they may receive.

The missal gives inexact instruction about the assembly's posture at communion time. In the United States the faithful are to kneel after the Lamb of God, unless the bishop directs otherwise (GIRM 43). The universal instruction is that the faithful remain standing throughout the distribution of communion, putting them in a posture of respect for the entire rite and uniting themselves with other communicants by adopting the same position.

However, many Catholics return to their place and kneel, promoting a time of private adoration. Singing at communion is "to express the spiritual union of the communicants by means of the unity of their voices, to show gladness of heart, and to bring out more clearly the 'communitarian' character of the procession to receive the Eucharist" (GIRM 86). This is hard to achieve when the faithful return to their places and kneel.

A careful analysis shows that the GIRM in the United States tells the faithful to kneel after the Lamb of God, but never when to stand. Each communicant stands to enter the communion line. In some parishes the faithful kneel after the Lamb of God while the priest and ministers receive communion, but then stand as the faithful receive. This presents a clearer visual image of the communion of the faithful, rather than their individual devotion.

All may sit for a period of thanksgiving during the sacred silence that follows communion (GIRM 43). In practice, many of the faithful do not sit until the priest sits. They wait for him to place the reserved sacrament back in the tabernacle, purify the vessels, and return to his chair.

Some parishes have reconceived the reposition of hosts in the tabernacle as a ritual of its own. If a deacon returns them, for example, the priest and ministers may turn to watch. In some cases multiple ministers genuflect before the tabernacle door is closed. In some parishes the turning of the key in the tabernacle door—and the clink the action emits—cues them to sit.

The actual rubric says something else: "if appropriate, [the faithful] may sit or kneel during the period of sacred silence after Communion" (GIRM 43). The change of posture does not happen when the priest sits nor when the tabernacle door is closed. It takes place "after Communion." The missal envisions that the faithful have stood throughout the distribution of communion as an expression of their union in Christ, and that they sit together when *communion* is over.

As with its instructions about reverences during Mass (GIRM 274) and the distribution of communion during Mass (85), the missal pays little attention to the tabernacle during the course of the Mass. It emphasizes the altar and the act of receiving communion. It calls for the full, conscious, active participation of the people in the parts of the Mass, not the full, conscious adoration of the people throughout the Mass.

The relocation of the tabernacle off its preconciliar placement atop the altar signaled the purpose of the altar as the source of sacrifice and communion. However, in many ways the practice in Catholic churches adopts the unsupportable notion that the reserved sacrament takes precedence over the shared sacrament, even during Mass.

Summary

Participating at Mass is the heart of Catholic eucharistic spirituality. Nonetheless, that center precipitates a series of devotional exercises that sustain believers in the good practice of faith. Catholics believe that Christ is truly present in the Eucharistic species, and that his presence endures among them even after the celebration of the Mass. That sets into motion a series of practices and customs celebrating and honoring the Blessed Sacrament.

Catholics obtain the greatest benefit from eucharistic reservation if they have participated fully in eucharistic communion at Mass. Nourished by the Eucharist, they continue their devotion with other exercises that derive from belief in the enduring real presence of the risen Christ in the consecrated hosts reserved after communion. The greatest treasure in the Church provides an unfailing source of spiritual nourishment.

The eucharistic revival in the United States stirred up a renewed commitment to belief in the real presence of Christ. It promoted opportunities for participating in Holy Communion at Mass and for worshiping the reserved Sacrament. Those who believe that Christ is truly present feel revived in the celebration of the Eucharist and compelled to honor the enduring presence of the risen Christ after the conclusion of Mass. This is possible through eucharistic reservation. Faithful Catholics take advantage of eucharistic reservation in various ways:

- They notify the pastor when a family or friend is dying so that a priest or another minister may bring Viaticum.

When the minister arrives, they participate in this ceremony, joining in the prayers and offering peace and support to the one they love who is about to lose their earthly life.

- They receive Holy Communion outside Mass at appropriate times, especially when a priest is not available to them. They keep the ministry of priests in their prayerful intentions.
- They spend time in adoration before the tabernacle or before the exposed Blessed Sacrament in a monstrance. During those periods, they pray for the needs of the world, listen to Scripture, join in singing, and develop their friendship with Christ. In this spirit, they prepare themselves for the next opportunity to receive Holy Communion at Mass.
- They join eucharistic processions and congresses. Participating in public expressions of their faith, they experience personal renewal and the thrill of evangelization.

The enduring presence of Christ in the eucharistic mystery supplies imperfect opportunities for receiving communion outside Mass and meaningful opportunities for worship. Even beyond the years of a eucharistic revival, these rituals help Catholics establish a balanced spirituality as they frequently give thanks to God for the gift of Christ, the Bread of Life.